JEWISH ENCOUNTERS

Jonathan Rosen, General Editor

Jewish Encounters is a collaboration between Schocken and
Nextbook, a project devoted to the promotion of Jewish litera-
ture, culture, and ideas.

>nextbook

PUBLISHED

FORTHCOMING

When General Grant Expelled the Jews

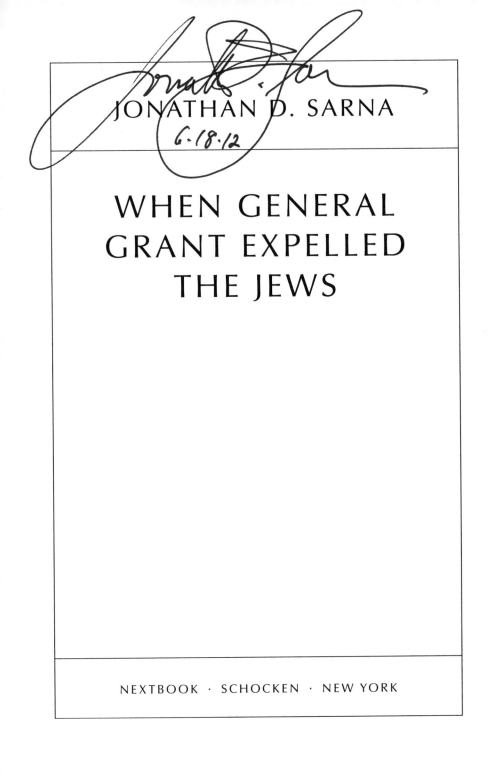

JONATHAN D. SARNA

6-18-12

WHEN GENERAL
GRANT EXPELLED
THE JEWS

NEXTBOOK · SCHOCKEN · NEW YORK

A portion of this work was previously published
in *Reform Judaism* (March 2012).

Library of Congress Cataloging-in-Publication Data
Sarna, Jonathan D.
    When General Grant expelled the Jews / Jonathan D. Sarna.
    p. cm.
    Includes index.
    ISBN 978-0-8052-4279-9
    1. United States—History—Civil War, 1861–1865—
Jews.   2. Grant, Ulysses S. (Ulysses Simpson), 1822–1885—
Political and social views.   3. Grant, Ulysses S. (Ulysses
Simpson), 1822–1885—Military leadership.   4. Jews—
Southern States—History—19th century.   5. United
States—Ethnic relations—History—19th century.   I. Title.
    E468.9.S26 2012   973.70892'4—dc23   2011028572

www.schocken.com

Jacket image: *General Ulysses S. Grant*, between 1860 and 1870,
glass negative. Courtesy of the Library of Congress,
Washington, D.C.
Jacket design by Joe Montgomery
Map by Mapping Specialists

Printed in the United States of America
First Edition
2   4   6   8   9   7   5   3   1

To my parents, ז"ל

מוה"ר נחום מתתיהו ומרת חיה הדסה סרנה
מורי הראשונים לתולדות עם ישראל וערכיו

CONTENTS

INTRODUCTION

The subject of this book once placed my academic career in jeopardy. In 1982, as a young faculty member at Hebrew Union College–Jewish Institute of Religion in Cincinnati, I was invited to deliver a talk before the institution's board of overseers. This was an important "rite of passage" for a new faculty member, and I was determined to prove myself. Since my lecture more or less coincided with the 120th anniversary of Ulysses S. Grant's General Orders No. 11 expelling "Jews as a class" from his war zone, I decided to take that infamous 1862 order as my subject. "No single act or word, let alone edict of another president or federal official, in all of American history, compares with the Grant order for rank generalization, harshness, or physical consequences," a standard reference source taught.[1] Using fresh material concerning the order that had become available in volume 16 of *The Papers of Ulysses S. Grant*, I prepared my remarks.

On the appointed day, my talk seemed to be going well until I broached the subject of smuggling. I stated that although Ulysses S. Grant had singled Jews out as smugglers, we now knew that smuggling was rampant throughout Grant's territory; it was by no means a Jewish monopoly. "In fact," I enthusiastically continued, "Grant's own father, Jesse Grant, was engaged in a clandestine scheme to move Southern cotton northward. His partners were Jewish clothing manufacturers named Harman, Henry, and Simon Mack."

A few chairs in the room shifted uneasily at that point, and my mentor, the pioneering American Jewish historian Jacob Rader Marcus, buried his face in his hands. That, I knew, spelled trouble. Clearly, I had just said something terribly wrong. Not knowing what the problem was, and fearing for the security of my job, I hobbled to the end of my lecture and invited questions.

An old man in the front row promptly raised his hand and rose to his feet. "My name is Mack," he memorably began. I later learned that his full name was Edgar Johnson Mack Jr.; he was known to his friends as Buddy. Looking me straight in the eye, he announced: "That was my great-grandfather you were talking about. . . . And," he continued after a long and dramatic pause, "it's all true."[2]

The room relaxed. Dr. Marcus looked up. And everybody smiled. My academic career was safe.

Since that memorable day, I have looked for an opportunity to expand upon the history of Ulysses S. Grant and the Jews. Although several academic articles and an important chapter in Bertram W. Korn's *American Jewry and the Civil War* discuss aspects of General Orders No. 11, its history, aftermath, and implications remain all-too-little known, even among students of the Civil War and biographers of Ulysses S. Grant. The Civil War sesquicentennial (which, naturally, also marks the 150th anniversary of Grant's order) seems an appropriate moment to set the record straight.

Americans today are surprised to learn that Ulysses S. Grant once expelled "Jews as a class" from his war zone. It seems incredible that Jews could be grouped together as part of a single "class" and ordered from their homes. So it is instructive to remember that, for all of America's much-vaunted distinctiveness, there was a brief moment, amid the horrors of the Civil War, when Old World prejudices displayed themselves. Some Jews at the time wondered whether their new homeland was coming to resemble antisemitic Europe at its worst.

In the end, only a few Jews were seriously affected by General Orders No. 11. A fortunate communications breakdown and Abraham Lincoln's prompt decision to revoke the order greatly limited its impact. When Lincoln declared that he did not "like to hear a class or nationality condemned on account of a few sinners," Jews felt reassured. In short order, attention returned to the battlefield, where, within a year, Grant's victory at Vicksburg elevated him to a national hero.

Like any trauma, however, General Orders No. 11 turned out to have lingering effects. In the short term, it brought to the surface deep-seated fears that, in the wake of the Emancipation Proclamation, Jews might replace Blacks as the nation's most despised minority. Some Jewish leaders explicitly feared that freedom for slaves would spell trouble for Jews.

Later on, in 1868, when Grant ran for president, the memory of General Orders No. 11 sparked passionate debates between Jews who extolled Grant as a national hero and those who reviled him as a latter-day Haman, an enemy of the Jews. The issue thrust Jews, for the first time in American history, into the center of the political maelstrom. The excruciating question that Jewish Republicans faced—should they vote for a party they considered bad for the country just to avoid voting for a man who had been bad to the Jews?—prefigured a central conundrum of Jewish politics. Never before had a Jewish issue played so prominent a role in any presidential campaign.

Still later, during the eight years of Grant's presidency, memories of General Orders No. 11 surfaced repeatedly. Eager to prove that he was above prejudice, Grant appointed more Jews to public office than had any of his predecessors and, in the name of human rights, he extended unprecedented support to persecuted Jews in Russia and Romania. Time and again, partly as a result of his enlarged vision of what it meant to be an American and partly in order to live down General Orders No. 11, Grant consciously worked to assist Jews and secure them equality.

Nevertheless, the memory of what his wife, Julia, called "that obnoxious order" continued to haunt Grant up to his death in 1885. Especially when he was in the company of Jews, the sense that in expelling them he had failed to live up to his own high standards of behavior, and to the Constitution that he had sworn to uphold, gnawed at him. He apologized for the order publicly and repented of it privately. He consciously excluded any mention of it from his acclaimed *Memoirs*. He gloried in the fact that, on his deathbed, Jews numbered among those who visited with him and prayed for his recovery.

The story of General Orders No. 11 and its lingering impact fills in a missing and revealing "Jewish" chapter in the biography of Ulysses S. Grant. But it also does much more than that, for the order and its aftermath also shed new light on one of the most tumultuous eras in American history, the era of the Civil War and Reconstruction. During these years—America's "Second Founding," as one historian terms it—the definition of what America is and the determination of who "we the people" should include convulsed the country.3 Most of the debate naturally centered on the status of African Americans but, more than generally recognized, there was likewise substantial debate concerning the Jews. Though they formed far less than 1 percent of the population at that time, Jews were the most significant non-Christian immigrant group in the nation and their numbers had been increasing rapidly—from about 15,000 in 1840 to some 150,000 on the eve of the Civil War. General Orders No. 11 implied that these Jews formed a separate "class" of Americans, distinct from their neighbors, and subject, especially when suspicions of smuggling fell upon them, to collective forms of punishment, including expulsion. The National Reform Association, which was particularly active during the 1870s, went further, seeking to "declare the nation's allegiance to Jesus Christ and its acceptance of the moral laws of the Christian religion, and so indicate that this is a Christian nation."4 A "religious" amendment, proposed repeatedly during the Grant years, looked to write Christianity directly into the Constitution itself.

Against this background, Ulysses S. Grant's surprising embrace of Jews during his presidency takes on new significance. Through his appointments and policies, Grant rejected calls for a "Christian nation" and embraced Jews as insiders in America, part of "we the people." During his administration, Jews achieved heightened status on the national scene. Judaism won recognition (at least from him) as a faith coequal to Protestantism and Catholicism. Anti-Jewish prejudice declined, and Jews looked forward optimistically to a liberal epoch characterized by sensitivity to human rights and interreligious cooperation. In the president's mind, a direct parallel existed between the treatment of Blacks under Reconstruction and the treatment of Jews. He sought to create new opportunities for members of both minority groups.

Reconstruction proved to be an "unfinished revolution" for African Americans, and so it was (albeit not nearly to the same extent) for Jews.[5] In 1877, the very year that Grant left the White House, his friend, banker Joseph Seligman, was excluded from the Grand Union Hotel as an "Israelite." Four years later, the great Reform Jewish leader Rabbi Isaac Mayer Wise complained that "we poor optimists are sadly disappointed and made false prophets."[6] By 1897, Professor Richard Gottheil of Columbia University felt that "gradually, but surely, we are being forced back into a physical and moral ghetto . . . our social lines run as far apart from those of our neighbors as they did in the worst days of our European degradation."[7] Across the United States, antisemitic restrictions and quotas led to a substantial decline in Jews' social status. The "golden age" of the Grant years had, by then, become a distant memory.

Readers today who grew up hearing squalid tales of Ulysses S. Grant's drunkenness, incompetence, and antisemitism will be surprised to learn that Jews had once viewed him more positively. Jews who lived during Grant's own lifetime, however, would have been unsurprised. They had watched Grant rehabilitate himself with the Jewish community and were familiar with his many Jewish friends and admirers. As a result, they participated wholeheartedly in the national mourning that followed his death in 1885, and later in the dedication of his tomb. They did so, in spite of General Orders No. 11, for they recognized, as Rabbi Isaac Mayer Wise noted at the time, that Grant had "often repented" of his order and "that the wise also fail."[8]

In recent years, a thoroughgoing reevaluation of Ulysses S. Grant has taken place. "Though much of the public and even some historians haven't yet heard the news," historian Sean Wilentz observed in the *New York Times*, "the vindication of Ulysses S. Grant is well under way. I expect that before too long Grant will be returned to the standing he deserves—not only as the military savior of the Union but also as one of the great presidents of his era, and possibly one of the greatest in all American history."[9] Tellingly, a letter to the editor dissented, recalling Grant's anti-Jewish actions during the Civil War.[10] This book, in a sense, is the answer to that letter writer. It places General Orders No. 11 within the larger context of Grant's career.

In the end, General Orders No. 11 greatly strengthened America's Jewish community. The successful campaign to overturn the order made Jews more self-confident. The tempestuous 1868 election taught them much about politics, and about the power—real and perceived—of a well-organized minority group. The fact that Ulysses S. Grant selected, for the first time, a Jewish adviser, appointed a series of Jews to public office, and attended the dedication of a synagogue further enhanced Jews' self-confidence. So did America's successful interventions on behalf of persecuted Jews in Russia and Romania.

It is always easy to exaggerate the political impact of a religious or ethnic minority, and Jews would have many occasions in the post-Grant years to learn the limits of their ability to win political appointments and effect public policy. Nevertheless, General Orders No. 11 marked a turning point in American Jewish history. Paradoxically, Ulysses S. Grant's order expelling the Jews set the stage for their empowerment.

When General Grant Expelled the Jews

1

General Orders No. 11

Cesar Kaskel's faith in America was wavering. Born in the town of Rawitsch, then part of Prussia, he, like tens of thousands of other young Jews in the 1850s, had left home and endured a long, perilous voyage across the Atlantic in hopes of establishing himself in business in the United States. Opportunities in Prussia were circumscribed for Jews, owing to domestic unrest, a failing economy, and severe legal limitations on where they could live and what kinds of occupations they could pursue. America, Kaskel had heard, was different. Dispatches in the German-Jewish press and letters received from earlier immigrants reported that in America opportunity was unlimited and freedom guaranteed to people of all faiths—Jews included. That guarantee, Kaskel now feared, had been voided.

Moving to Paducah, Kentucky, in 1858, Kaskel imagined he had found just the opportunity he had been looking for. The newly incorporated city, located on the Ohio River below the mouth of the Tennessee River and fifty miles up from the Mississippi, was booming. Its population grew exponentially, reaching almost five thousand residents by the Civil War. A timely investment by city fathers in the stock of the New Orleans and Ohio Railway brought Paducah excellent rail connections and a growing volume of trade. Kaskel and his business partner, merchant Solomon Greenbaum, looked to participate in this prodigious growth. They set themselves up in business.[1]

Two years later, in 1860, a Kentucky native son, Abraham Lincoln, was

Cesar Kaskel

elected the sixteenth president of the United States. Fewer than 1 percent of Kentucky voters supported him. Fearing that the new president and his party threatened slavery and the distinctive character of life in the South, seven Southern states, led by South Carolina, seceded to form the Confederate States of America. When the Confederacy bombarded the coastal fortification of Fort Sumter at the entrance to Charleston harbor on April 12, 1861, forcing it to surrender, war broke out. Once President Lincoln called for troops to quell the rebellion, four more states, including Virginia, joined the Confederacy, while four states on the border between the North and the South, including Kentucky, did not.

The Civil War disrupted economic life in Paducah and changed Kaskel's life for the worse. The North began restricting Southern trade with Paducah as early as June 12, 1861, seeking to place economic pressure on the Confederacy. On September 6, Ulysses S. Grant and his troops captured and occupied the city, further restricting its trade with the South. The state of Kentucky declared itself neutral in the war, but Grant believed that the majority of Paducah's citizens "would have much preferred the presence of the other army."[2] Be that as it may, at least some of the city's thirty-odd Jews publicly supported the Union's cause. Cesar Kaskel was one of them; he served as vice president of the Paducah Union League Club. His younger brother, Julius, operated as a recruiter for the Union army.[3]

The disruption of free trade in Paducah created bountiful opportunities for speculators and smugglers, who always find ways to profit from wartime shortages and imbalances between supply and demand. While merchants like Kaskel burnished their pro-Union credentials in hopes of obtaining precious trade permits, officials entrusted with governing trade in and out of the city found backhanded ways to line their own pockets; so did many soldiers. In short order, public corruption rose, mutual trust declined, and recriminations abounded. As is so often the case in such circumstances, suspicion fell particularly upon the Jews, long stereotyped in Christian culture as being financially unscrupulous. Jews became the focus for much of the hatred and mistrust that the war unleashed within the city. Even though few in number in Paducah, they played an outsized role in business and trade, and as immigrants they were easily marked by their European accents and foreign ways. Unionists and Confederates alike doubted their loyalties—partly because they doubted the loyalty of

Occupation of Paducah by General Grant

all Jews and partly because Jews nationwide were known to be on both sides of the struggle. Many therefore assumed, even in the absence of supporting evidence, that "secessionists and Jews" were engaged in "rascally conduct" in Paducah and that widespread smuggling was carried out "as usual chiefly by Jews."[4]

Tense as conditions were in Paducah, nothing had prepared Cesar Kaskel for the events of December 28, 1862, and his agitated response to them was understandable. Pursuing his business, in his words, as a "peaceable, law abiding citizen,"[5] he was suddenly summoned, on a Sunday, to report "immediately" to Paducah's provost marshal, Captain L. J. Waddell. There he was handed the following order banishing him from the city:

OFFICE OF PROVOST MARSHAL
Paducah, Ky., December 28, 1862
C. J. Kaskel—Sir: In pursuance of General Order No 11, issued from General Grant's headquarters, you are hereby ordered to leave the city of Paducah, Kentucky, within twenty-four hours after receiving this order.
By order,
L. J. WADDELL,
Captain and Provost Marshal

Kaskel was not the only person ordered to leave. As he heatedly informed the newspapers, anyone "born of Jewish parents" was likewise expelled: "nearly thirty other gentlemen, mostly married, all respectable men, and old residents of Paducah, two of whom have served their country . . . and all loyal to the Government." Women and children were expelled too, and in the confusion—so it was recalled years later—one baby was almost forgotten, and two dying women had to be left behind in the care of neighbors. Historian John E. L. Robertson preserves a (dubious) local tradition that citizens of Paducah hid some Jews to prevent their being sent away. "One soldier," he reports, "is said to have knocked on the door of a Jew and demanded, 'What are you?' The resident of the house answered truthfully, 'Tailor.' To which the none-too-bright soldier replied, 'Sorry to bother you, Mr. Taylor, but I'm looking for Jews.' "[6]

Cesar Kaskel quickly came to understand that Captain Waddell, in expelling him from his home, was simply following orders. The decision to evict Jews from the vast war zone under the command of General Ulysses S. Grant—known as the "Department of the Tennessee," but actually stretching from northern Mississippi to Cairo, Illinois, and from the Mississippi River to the Tennessee River—appeared in a document entitled "General Orders No. 11" issued under Grant's own signature eleven days earlier, on December 17. Waddell handed Kaskel a copy of Grant's scarcely-to-be-believed order, and he wisely preserved it. Subsequently described as "the most sweeping anti-Jewish regulation in all American history,"[7] it read as follows:

GENERAL ORDERS, } HDQRS. 13TH A.C. DEPT. OF THE TENN.,
 NO. 11.   }   *Holly Springs, December 17, 1862.*

The Jews, as a class violating every regulation of trade established by the Treasury Department and also department orders, are hereby expelled from the department within twenty-four hours from the receipt of this order.

Post commanders will see that all of this class of people be furnished passes and required to leave, and any one returning after such notification will be arrested and held in confinement until an opportunity occurs of sending them out as prisoners, unless furnished with permit from headquarters.

No passes will be given these people to visit headquarters for the purpose of making personal application for trade permits.

By order of Maj. Gen. U. S. Grant:

JNO. A. RAWLINS,
Assistant Adjutant-General.[*]

---

[*] This is the "official text" of the order, issued at Grant's field headquarters in Holly Springs and preserved in the *Official Records of the War of the Rebellion*, series I, vol. 17

Kaskel instantly decided to fight the order expelling him from his home. His faith in America, after all, hung in the balance. There was, however, nobody of authority in Paducah with whom to fight. Nor, even had he tried, could he have appealed to General Grant. Less than seventy-two hours after issuing General Orders No. 11, Grant's forces at Holly Springs had been surprised by thirty-five hundred Confederate raiders led by Major General Earl Van Dorn. Since Grant himself was far from the scene, and the commanding officer, Robert C. Murphy, was "out at some entertainment" that made him, in the delicate words of a contemporary journalist, "a trifle over bold," the results proved devastating: "Holly Springs was surrounded by rebel cavalry and surrendered without resistance; over a million rations burned, several hundred bales of cotton destroyed . . . and 2,000 troops [captured]."[8] Simultaneous raids to the north by troops of the dreaded Confederate cavalryman General Nathan Bedford Forrest inflicted significant damage and tore up fifty miles of railroad and telegraph lines.

Communications between Grant's headquarters and the military command were disrupted for weeks by these surprise attacks. As a result, news of Grant's order expelling the Jews spread slowly and did not reach army headquarters in a timely fashion—sparing many Jews who might

----

(part 2), 424. Another text, issued from Grant's department headquarters at Oxford, Mississippi, is designated "General Orders No. 12" and carries slightly different wording. A third text, with other minor differences in wording, was published in the *New York Herald*, January 5, 1863. A fourth text, with still other variants, is found in a handwritten copy of a U.S. military telegraph sent to Brigadier General Mason Brayman and preserved in the Chicago History Museum (see illustration opposite). The discrepancy in numbering was caused by the discovery that a completely unrelated "General Orders No. 11" was issued by the Department of the Tennessee at La Grange, Tennessee, on November 26. While the text issued at Oxford therefore corrected the numbering and slightly improved the language of the order, "General Orders No. 11" remained the name by which the order was known. For the corrected text issued at Oxford, see *The Papers of Ulysses S. Grant*, vol. 7, p. 50. Note that the official text properly uses the plural form ("General Orders"), since generals inevitably issued many orders. Unofficially, though, the singular form, "General Order No. 11," was common.

Text of General Orders No. 11 telegraphed to Brigadier General Mason Brayman

otherwise have been banished. Nor did remonstrations against the order reach Grant. To overturn General Orders No. 11, Kaskel would have to appeal to superiors in Washington.

Following time-tested traditions of Jewish politics, Kaskel began by appealing to the highest governmental power available. Long experience with persecution had persuaded Jews "that their ultimate safety and welfare could be entrusted neither to the erratic benevolence of their gentile neighbors nor to the caprice of local authorities."⁹ Kaskel appealed instead to the president of the United States. Within just a few hours of being served with the order of expulsion, and without any known assistance

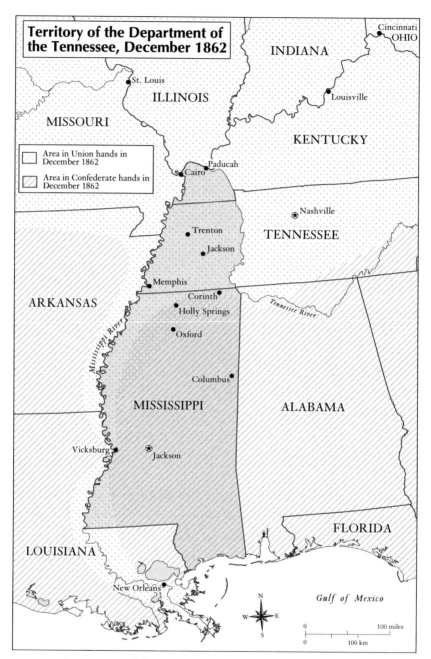

Territory of the Department of the Tennessee, December 1862

Area in Union hands in December 1862

Area in Confederate hands in December 1862

Cincinnati
OHIO
INDIANA
St. Louis
ILLINOIS
Louisville
MISSOURI
KENTUCKY
Paducah
Cairo
Nashville
Trenton
TENNESSEE
Jackson
Memphis
ARKANSAS
Corinth
Holly Springs
Tennessee River
Oxford
Columbus
MISSISSIPPI
ALABAMA
Vicksburg
Jackson
Mississippi River
FLORIDA
LOUISIANA
New Orleans
Gulf of Mexico
N
W—E
S
0   100 miles
0   100 km

Department of the Tennessee, December 1862. Grant's forces
were preparing to move on Vicksburg, then in Confederate hands.

from leading Jews of the time, Kaskel, his brother Julius, merchant Daniel Wolff, and Wolff's two brothers, Marcus and Alexander, dispatched a joint telegram to Abraham Lincoln at the White House. In it, they briefly set forth the terms of General Orders No. 11, described themselves as "good and loyal citizens of the United States," and pronounced themselves—as Americans—"greatly insulted and outraged by this inhuman order, the carrying out of which would be the grossest violation of the Constitution, and our rights as good citizens under it." They pointed to the larger implications of Grant's order, which, if allowed to stand, would stigmatize Jews "as outlaws before the whole world." They appealed to Lincoln for his "immediate attention to this enormous outrage on all law and humanity" and asked for his "effectual and immediate interposition." With their own imminent deportation uppermost in their minds, they requested, in the final sentence of their costly telegram, that "immediate instructions . . . be sent to the commander of this post." Three times in three sentences they repeated the word "immediate." They were desperate.[10]

Lincoln, in all likelihood, never saw this telegram.[11] He was busy preparing to issue the Emancipation Proclamation (January 1, 1863), freeing Confederate-held slaves as "an act of justice, warranted by the Constitution." The irony of his freeing the slaves while Grant was expelling the Jews was not lost on some contemporaries. The *Memphis Daily Bulletin* published the two documents, one above the other.[12] The juxtaposition of these events, as we shall see, also shaped the responses of several Jewish leaders to Grant's order. They feared that Jews would replace Blacks as the nation's stigmatized minority. But on December 31, when the telegram was read by General-in-Chief Henry Halleck, all of this was far from anybody's mind. Not being familiar with Kaskel, and having no knowledge of the events that the telegram described, Halleck, with characteristic caution, sought to obtain more information. "Respectfully referred to Gen[era]l Grant for report," he noted in his endorsement. By the time Grant reported, two weeks later, the order had been discussed in the halls of Congress.[13]

Ulysses S. Grant,
about 1860

Kaskel, in the meanwhile, did not wait patiently. His telegram to Lincoln unanswered, he climbed aboard the steamship *Charley Bowen*, which would carry him and other Jews out of Grant's department, and hastily penned a strongly worded account of their banishment for distribution to the press. The Associated Press picked up the story, and it appeared, dated December 30, 1862, in a number of newspapers, headlined, in one case, "Expulsion of Jews from General Grant's Department—The Circumstances Stated and Documents Quoted." As a merchant, Kaskel intuitively understood the power of public opinion. He concluded his account, effectively, with a plea for help: "On my way to Washington, in order to get this most outrageous and inhuman order of Major General Grant countermanded, I ask you, gentlemen, to lend the powerful aid of the press to the suffering cause of outraged humanity; to blot out as quick as possible this stain on our national honor, and to show the world that the

American people, as a nation, brand the author of that infamous order as unworthy of their respect and confidence."[14]

Kaskel passed through Cairo, Illinois, and probably Cincinnati on his Paul Revere–like ride to Washington.[15] He spread the word of Grant's order wherever he went. Armed with letters from Rabbi Max Lilienthal of Cincinnati and the prominent Cincinnati merchant Daniel Wolf, he hurried on. He was determined to do whatever it took to have Grant's order reversed and his faith in America restored.

While Kaskel made his way as quickly as he could to Washington, other Jewish leaders, alerted to the order, swung into action. The most important by far was Isaac Mayer Wise, Cincinnati's most prominent rabbi, the editor of the *Israelite*, the region's most widely read Jewish newspaper, and one of the country's leading proponents of Jewish religious reform. At forty-three, the hyperactive, somewhat contentious, and voluble rabbi was in the prime of his life. He had been in America for sixteen years, achieved mastery of the English language, and won friends in high places.

Rabbi Isaac Mayer Wise

Pragmatic, flexible, and politically savvy, he generally advocated compromise for the sake of unity both within the Jewish community and in the nation as a whole. Consequently, the "live and let live" policy of Democrats like Stephen A. Douglas strongly appealed to him, the policies of Abraham Lincoln and the Republican Party largely repelled him, and the "fanatical" abolitionists, some of whom displayed deep religious prejudice against Jews, frightened and alienated him. Residing opposite a border state, with "dear friends and near relations . . . in either section of the country," Wise favored peace and sectional self-determination to uphold the union, even if that meant acquiescing to slavery. When it came to the rights of Jews, though, he was uncompromising. He was a one-man Anti-Defamation League, chronicling antisemitic slurs and actions and doing all in his power to combat them.[16]

News of Grant's order first reached Wise independently of Kaskel. Jews expelled from Holly Springs, some of whom were compelled to trudge forty miles on foot to Memphis, communicated with him. Details of their experiences were somewhat garbled (an early report referred to Grant's order as "No. 29"), but the rabbi quickly understood that what had happened was an "outrage, without a precedent in American history." He urged all whom the order victimized to send him, without delay, "affidavits to this effect, made before a justice of the peace or a notary public, or publish them in other newspapers, and send us the publications." He insisted, as warriors against prejudice almost invariably do, that it was "everybody's business" to investigate the prejudicial order, since what had happened to Jews could happen to other spurned nationalities and religious communities, like the Irish or Catholics generally (in fact, they did face significant wartime prejudice, but never orders of expulsion). Most of all, he sought to rouse his own community to action:

> Israelites, citizens of the United States, you have been outraged, your rights as men and citizens trampled into the dust, your honor disgraced, as a class you have officially been degraded! It is your

duty, the duty of self-defense, your duty first to bring this matter clearly before the president of the United States and demand
redress, the satisfaction due to the citizen who has been mortified
and offended.[17]

Privately, though, Wise counseled caution. He worried, given the tem-
per of the times, that too strong a Jewish protest could backfire. In letters
to Secretary of War Edwin M. Stanton, he explained that "this is a time
of excitement and I do not wish to pour oil in the fire. I do not wish to
excite prejudices against military men, as they need all the confidence
of the people." Having spelled out for Stanton the substance of General
Orders No. II and the contents of "legal affidavits" recounting four different examples of Jews who were expelled from Grant's territory, barred
from entering it, or otherwise degraded because of the order, he called
upon Stanton "to make an end to this chicanery." He hinted that timely
action by the secretary of war would forestall the kinds of protests that
could only hinder the war effort.[18]

In a follow-up letter five days later, Wise revealed—as he did nowhere
else—that he personally opposed sending delegations to the president,
but that "notwithstanding my opposition, deputations from Louisville,
Ky, Paducah, Ky, Cincinnati and elsewhere have been appointed . . . and
I *must* go with them to Washington." He encouraged Stanton to move
quickly, "previous to the call of the committees." With Kaskel and so
many others en route to Washington, he faced a dilemma that many a
leader can empathize with. Those whom he had himself helped to bestir
now sought to move further and faster than he did, and he worried that
they might rush ahead and cause mischief.[19]

The other "deputations" preparing to descend upon Washington,
besides Kaskel, consisted of leaders and would-be leaders from across the
spectrum of Jewish life. How many planned to come is unknown, but
there were enough of them to catch the attention of journalists. "Deputations of Jews are arriving here to solicit the President to countermand or

Petition of Missouri B'nai B'rith to Abraham Lincoln,
January 5, 1863

modify the order of Gen. Grant excluding Israelites from his lines," one newspaper reported. With the American Jewish community decentralized and divided, many claimed to represent the Jewish community in America, but none did so with authority.[20]

The recently established and grandly titled Board of Delegates of American Israelites (its name echoing that of London Jewry's influential Board of Deputies), representing some twenty-five mostly East Coast congregations, was poised to send a deputation of notables to Washington. It closely followed events in the capital through the eyes of Adolphus Solomons, proprietor of the notable bookselling, printing, and publishing establishment

Philp & Solomons, close to the White House on Pennsylvania Avenue. The Board's leaders had called an emergency meeting and were discussing what to do when a reassuring telegram from Solomons brought word that they could stay home. The Board subsequently took far more credit than it was due for its response to Grant's order. Events overtook it.[21]

The Jewish fraternal organization B'nai B'rith, which boasted lodges across the United States, likewise geared up to lobby against Grant's order. An eloquent plea from the order's Missouri lodges, addressed to President Lincoln, insisted that Jews were a "class of *loyal* citizens," who had been "driven from their homes, deprived of their liberty, and injured in their property *without* having violated any law or regulation" and who were "sacrificing their lives and fortunes for the union and the suppression of this rebellion." It called upon the president "to annul that Order and to protect the liberties even of your humblest constituents." Attorney General Edward Bates, who forwarded this poignant document to Lincoln, expressed "no particular interest in the subject."[22] Lincoln, as we shall see, *was* interested, but needed no encouragement from humble Missouri constituents. Even before their petition was mailed, he had acted.

The B'nai B'rith petition remains valuable nevertheless, for it listed the locations where Grant's order had been enforced against Jews: "Holly Springs, Trenton, Corinth, Paducah, Jackson, and other places." These were not the major Jewish population centers in Grant's department; far more Jews lived in Memphis. Some 150,000 Jews, most of them new immigrants, lived in the United States as a whole at that time, at least 25,000 of them in the lands of the Confederacy. Yet where Grant's order might have led to the expulsion of thousands of Jews, it seems to have affected fewer than one hundred. Aside from Kaskel and his fellow Jews in Paducah, almost all those expelled were residents and traders in the vicinity of the main body of Grant's army, in northern Mississippi.[23]

To be sure, some were treated roughly. A "Mr. Silberman" from Chicago, temporarily in Holly Springs, was reportedly imprisoned for twelve hours just for the "crime" of seeking to telegraph General Grant to find out if the expulsion order he received was genuine. An unnamed young Jewish trader and his fiancée, traveling through Grant's department on their way east, described in New York's *Jewish Record* how they were detained, forbidden to change out of wet clothes, robbed of their horses and buggy, verbally abused, and also had one of their trunks burned and their pockets picked in the wake of the order. Their expulsion, if not their mistreatment, was explained by Brigadier General James Tuttle, commander of the Union garrison in Cairo, Illinois, with the utmost simplicity: "You are Jews, and . . . neither a benefit to the Union or Confederacy."[24]

As painful as these and parallel stories of Jewish mistreatment undoubtedly were, it is the widespread disregard of Grant's order in the large territory under his command that actually cries out for explanation. Part of the reason, we have seen, was the breakdown of communications following the attacks on Holly Springs. Some in Grant's department never saw General Orders No. 11, while others who asked questions before carrying the order out likely received no replies.

One obvious question that may have given commanders pause was whether the expulsion order applied to soldiers who were Jewish. Of the eight to ten thousand Jews who donned uniforms during the Civil War, many hundreds, in late 1862, were serving under Grant, including a lieutenant colonel named Marcus M. Spiegel and a captain of the Ohio Volunteer Cavalry named Philip Trounstine. According to the broadest interpretation of Grant's order ("The Jews, as a class . . . are hereby expelled from the Department"), they should all have been banished. Nobody is known to have interpreted the order that way, but the presence of Jews in the ranks may well have delayed the order's execution in some instances.[25]

At least four different officers did telegraph Grant to inquire as to whether his order applied to Jewish sutlers, the merchants and peddlers who followed the military camps selling tobacco, liquor, clothing, foodstuffs, and a wide range of other nonmilitary goods in stores on or near

Soldiers in camp visiting the sutler's store

the post, under license from the commander. The word "sutler" comes from a root meaning "to follow a mean or low occupation" (the word "soot" comes from the same cognate), and no doubt for that reason Jews, even back in Europe, had long been permitted to engage in it. As so often before, they were admitted into this less-than-respected trade and then hated all the more for practicing it. It was risky, unpopular, but nevertheless vital and lucrative work, and immigrant Jews with long experience in peddling, marketing, and extending credit took it up during the Civil War, several of them serving in the territory under Grant's command. If Jewish sutlers were expelled, commanders wondered, who would meet the day-to-day needs of the soldiers? While they waited for an answer, most commanders allowed their Jewish sutlers to keep on working.[26]

Finally, and most significantly, there is evidence that at least one commander refused to carry out Grant's order, believing it to be illegal. Isaac Mayer Wise, relying on information from Jews in the field, reported that

A. LINCOLN.

Abraham Lincoln, about 1863

General Jeremiah Cutler Sullivan "refused to execute Grant's order," on the grounds that "he thought he was an officer of the army and not of a church." Sullivan had himself worked as a lawyer and came from a family eminent in the law. His father was a justice of the Indiana Supreme Court and his brother, Algernon Sydney Sullivan, later cofounded the white-shoe New York law firm of Sullivan and Cromwell. This may have made the general especially sensitive to human rights abuses and those legal "niceties" too often overlooked (even in our day) on the field of battle. At the time of Grant's order, General Sullivan commanded the District of Jackson, Tennessee, and was busy repelling Brigadier General Nathan Bedford Forrest's marauders. So his instinctive refusal to carry out Grant's order is instructive. While additional evidence concerning those who refused to carry out Grant's order is lacking, Wise reports that Sullivan's principled resistance to the order was eventually broken: "He was forced after 4 days to enforce it."[27]

Cesar Kaskel, making his way as fast as he could to Washington, probably knew nothing about any of this. Arriving in the nation's capital just as the Sabbath was concluding on January 3—travel on the Jewish day of rest would have been sanctioned even by the most scrupulous authorities, given the nature of his mission—he called at once upon Cincinnati congressman John Addison Gurley. Gurley was a Republican, and though defeated in his 1862 bid for reelection, he had Jewish friends and supporters in Cincinnati and enjoyed ready access to the White House. The ousted congressman, with Kaskel in tow, sought an immediate audience with the president, and according to the likely embellished account published many years later, Lincoln "sent word that he was 'always glad to see his friends,' and shortly made his appearance." The president turned out to have no knowledge whatsoever of the order, for it had not reached Washington. According to an oft-quoted report, he resorted to biblical imagery in his interview with Kaskel, a reminder of how many nineteenth-century Americans linked Jews to ancient Israel, and America to the Promised Land:

LINCOLN: And so the children of Israel were driven from the happy land of Canaan?

KASKEL: Yes, and that is why we have come unto Father Abraham's bosom, asking protection.

LINCOLN: And this protection they shall have at once.[28]

Even if (as seems likely) no such conversation actually took place, Lincoln did instantly command the general in chief of the army, Henry Halleck, to countermand General Orders No. 11. He reassured Kaskel that he had nothing further to worry about and could return home. Halleck, for his part, still had trouble believing in the authenticity of the original order, though Kaskel had shown him a copy. Consequently, in writing to Grant, he chose his words carefully. "If such an order has been issued," his telegram of January 4 read, "it will be immediately revoked." Two days later, several urgent telegrams went out from Grant's headquarters in obedience to that demand: "By direction of the General in Chief of the Army at Washington," they read, "the General Order from these Head Quarters expelling Jews from this Department is hereby revoked."[29]

Kaskel, by then, was safely home in Paducah, having reached there before the revocation became known. When the post commander demanded to know by whose orders he had returned, Kaskel, even years later, recalled his vigorous and definitive reply: "By order of the President of the United States."[30] Thanks to Lincoln, his faith in the country had been restored.

Unofficially, Halleck's assistant adjutant general, John C. Kelton, explained to Grant the president's central problem with General Orders No. 11: "It excluded a whole class, instead of certain obnoxious individuals." Sixteen days later, Halleck followed this up with an official explanation, likely prepared for public consumption:

> It may be proper to give you some explanation of the revocation of your order expelling all Jews from your department. The President has no objection to your expelling traitors and Jew peddlers, which, I suppose, was the object of your order; but, as it in terms proscribed an entire religious class, some of whom are fighting in our ranks, the President deemed it necessary to revoke it.[31]

News of the revocation soon spread. Newspapers across the country carried the story. Adolphus Solomons personally confirmed the news in a jubilant telegram to the Board of Delegates ("Feeling happy to have it in my power to attest the promptitude of our Government in countermanding the ill-liberal and un-lawful 'order' of Genl. Grant"). Delegations of Jews from Cincinnati and Louisville, on their way to Washington to lobby against General Orders No. 11, also heard the news, probably from the *Philadelphia Inquirer*, which carried it in its issue of January 6. Rather than turning around in Philadelphia and going home, though, they decided to continue onward and thank the president personally for what he had done.[32]

Owing once again to Congressman James A. Gurley's influential ties to the White House, the Cincinnati and Louisville delegations quickly got in to see Lincoln—so quickly, indeed, that the delegates, including rabbis, lawyers, and one of Grant's victims, Abraham Goldsmith of Paducah, had no time to change out of their traveling clothes. Isaac Mayer Wise, who participated in the meeting, wrote a widely circulated account of what transpired. Though he had not previously been one of the president's acolytes, he was now deeply impressed. Lincoln, he reported, "knows of no distinction between Jew and Gentile." In addition, he "feels no prejudice against any nationality," and "by no means will allow that a citizen in any wise be wronged on account of his place of birth or religious confession." "To condemn a class," he quoted Lincoln as declaring, thereby turning Grant's order practically on its head, "is, to say the least, to wrong the good with the bad. I do not like to hear a class or nationality condemned on account of a few sinners."[33]

2

"Jews as a Class"

Senator Lazarus Powell of Kentucky was shocked by the expulsion of his Jewish constituents from Paducah. A lawyer, former state governor, and staunch Democrat, he had remained in the Senate despite pressure to join the Confederacy; he would not abandon the Constitution. While he vigorously opposed the Civil War and defended slavery on constitutional grounds, he also became one of the Senate's foremost defenders of civil liberties in wartime—for citizens, not for Black slaves. Early in the war, he delivered a celebrated address condemning the suspension of habeas corpus by Abraham Lincoln. "If you allow the Executive or any other officer to suspend this great writ," he declared, "who is it who is secure in his person or his liberty?" Later, he condemned the arrests without trial that became all too commonplace in the Civil War. According to him, some five thousand of his Kentucky constituents had been so imprisoned, in violation of "the plainest provision of the Constitution." He even rose to defend himself in 1862, when his Republican opponent from Kentucky sought to have him expelled from his seat in the Senate on grounds of disloyalty; he survived by a vote of 28 to 11. Insisting upon his duty to speak truth to power, and deaf to the argument that rights might need to be suspended in the short term so that the Union might survive for the long term, Powell declared it his obligation as a senator "to arraign the President and all others in authority who violate the Constitution of my country."[1]*

* U. S. Grant's view was different. "The right to resist or suppress rebellion is as inherent as the right of self defense, and as natural as the right of an individual to preserve

Lazarus W. Powell

So it was that Powell mounted the Senate's rostrum on January 5, 1863, to propose a resolution condemning Ulysses S. Grant's General Orders No. 11 as "illegal, tyrannical, cruel and unjust."[2] Two days later, a parallel resolution was introduced into the House of Representatives by Ohio congressman George H. Pendleton, a Peace Democrat of Virginia background, who likewise stressed "strict adherence" to the Constitution. The order having been revoked by the president, however, the critical question of civil liberties in wartime that both men sought to highlight rapidly dissolved into party politics: Democrats attacked Grant; Republicans defended him. Grant's longtime friend and chief congressional promoter, the Radical Republican Elihu B. Washburne of Galena, Illinois, moved to table the House resolution. He condemned it for censuring "one of our best generals without a hearing." Privately, in a letter to Abraham Lincoln, he described Grant's order as "the wisest order yet made by a

his life when in jeopardy," he wrote in his *Memoirs*. "The Constitution was therefore in abeyance for the time being, so far as it in any way affected the progress and termination of the war." *Memoirs and Selected Letters: Personal Memoirs of U. S. Grant, Selected Letters 1839–1865* (New York: Library of America, 1990), 749.

military command, and . . . necessary." He begged him not to rescind the order, for "there are two sides to this question." Lincoln, of course, had already acted, but thanks in good part to Washburne's vigorous defense of Grant, the House resolution went nowhere.[3]

In the Senate, though, Lazarus Powell proved resolute. In a major speech on the Senate floor on January 9, he pushed forward his resolution as necessary, "particularly at this time, when the constitutional rights of the citizens are being stricken down and trodden under foot throughout the entire country by the executive and military power." Declaring that there was "no excuse for General Grant . . . issuing the order," he reiterated that only those "who violated the law" should have been expelled, not "Jews as a class." He called upon his fellow senators to "administer to those in command of our armies the sternest rebuke for such flagrant outrages . . . to teach these military gentlemen that they are not thus to encroach on the civil and religious rights of the citizen, whether he be Jew or Gentile."[4]

Powell did not ultimately prevail. The Senate tabled his resolution by a vote of 30 to 7. But even the opposition offered no defense of Grant's order. "General Grant issued an order that I take it no man in the Senate approves," declared Massachusetts Republican Henry Wilson (who, ironically, later served as Grant's vice president). "The order excluding a whole class of men is utterly indefensible." Still, the order had been revoked and Jewish rights "promptly vindicated." So instead of rebuking one of the Union's best and most able generals, he, along with the majority of other senators, voted to "let the matter drop."[5]

The national press did not let the matter drop quite so quickly. Editorials continued to appear for at least another nine days. Generally speaking, the Republican newspapers supported Grant, whereas the Democratic ones opposed him. In cities with significant Jewish populations, like Cincinnati and New York, even newspapers sympathetic to Grant editorialized against his order. Elsewhere, a few newspapers sought to fuel the controversy. One groundlessly alleged that Jews were "arming themselves to resist further interference with their rights." Another scurrilously characterized Jews as "notorious" for "illegitimate . . . modes of making money" and "scavengers . . . of commerce." Yet the dominant message of editorial writers, even those sympathetic to Grant, was that Jews should be treated as individuals and not collectively as a "class." "No offense can be committed by individuals, which will justify the singling out of a whole class," the habitually Democratic *Cincinnati Enquirer* thundered; "there are black sheep in every flock." The pro-Republican *Cincinnati Commercial*, meanwhile, called upon Grant to "word his orders so as not to do injustice and injury to 'a class.'" The *New York Times*, not yet a Jewish-owned paper, devoted three long paragraphs to this same theme, reminding its readers, "All swindlers are not Jews. All Jews are not swindlers." Years later this same formulation (substituting other words for "swindlers") would be used to defend Jews against those who stereotyped them as "radicals," "Communists," and "financial crooks." The newspaper concluded, as so many others had, that "men cannot be condemned and punished as a class, without gross violence to our free institutions."[6]

While newspapers soon moved on to other subjects, such as the Emancipation Proclamation, General Orders No. 11 continued to pose deeply troubling questions to America's Jews. Many of those tar-

Isaac Leeser

geted by Grant's order, after all, were immigrants like Cesar Kaskel. They had left home and crossed the ocean in the cherished belief that America was different, for it treated Jews as individuals and placed no special restrictions upon them. Now they had cause to wonder: Was it really so different? Did America's guarantee of "liberty and justice for all" exclude "Jews as a class"? America's greatest hero, George Washington, had promised Jews that the "Government of the United States . . . gives to bigotry no sanction, to persecution no assistance." How, then, to explain Grant's order? True, Abraham Lincoln had promptly seen it revoked, but why had Grant escaped all punishment? And why had Congress "let the matter drop" rather than censuring him?

"We are still in bondage," Isaac Leeser explained simply. The foremost advocate of Orthodox Judaism in America, and editor of America's oldest Jewish publication, *The Occident*, Leeser, who lived in Philadelphia and maintained close ties to relatives in the Confederate capital of Richmond, published a rambling ten-thousand-word essay ("a greater length than ever we permitted ourself since our first appearance") in response to Grant's expulsion order. Entitled "On Persecution," it made clear to American Jews that they were still in exile, subjected, like all other Diaspora Jews, to the "decrees of those in power, who are not restrained by any feeling of humanity and justice from inflicting injury on us." America, Leeser lamented, had lost regard for the "rights of all" in the decade prior to Grant's order. "Should the deterioration proceed in the same ratio for the next fifty years," he despaired, "despotism, military and civil, may naturally succeed to overthrow a rotten State which has ceased to be free except in name."[7]

Leeser viewed Grant's order as evidence of "deep-seated prejudice," a "latent sentiment inimical to Judaism" spreading throughout the country. He was not wrong. The tensions and frustrations of war, which frequently found their outlet in persecutions of Catholics and African Americans during the Civil War years, likewise anathematized Jews. One student of the subject, historian Bertram W. Korn, has concluded that anti-Jewish

Judah P. Benjamin

prejudice was actually "far greater in articulation, repetition, frequency, and in action too, than had ever before been directed against Jews in America." These prejudices were heightened by the prominence of several Jews, notably President Jefferson Davis's right-hand man and cabinet secretary, Judah P. Benjamin, in the ranks of the Confederacy. The *Boston Transcript*, for one, took early notice of the fact that Benjamin and other Jews were contributing to the Confederate cause. Generalizing from the few to the many, it denounced the entire "stiffnecked generation" of the "Children of Israel" for taking the "lead in attempting to destroy a Constitution which has been to them an Ark of refuge and safety." No fewer than five distinguished public figures, including three U.S. senators (one of whom, Andrew Johnson, later became president of the United States), are likewise known to have pilloried Benjamin specifically as a Jew. One of them, Senator Benjamin F. Wade of Ohio, memorably described him as an "Israelite with Egyptian principles." Other Jews, too, were almost always identified as such when their names appeared in the public press. Like Black Americans, their distinctiveness defined them.[8]

Fault for many of the other evils inevitably associated with war—

smuggling, speculating, price gouging, swindling, and producing "shoddy" merchandise for the military—was similarly laid upon the doorstep of "the Jews." Indeed, "Jews" came to personify the foulest ills of wartime capitalism. They bore disproportionate blame for badly produced uniforms, poorly firing weapons, inedible foodstuffs, and other substandard merchandise that corrupt contractors supplied to the war effort and sutlers marketed to the troops. In the eyes of many Americans (including some in the military), *all* traders, smugglers, sutlers, and wartime profiteers were "sharp-nosed" Jews, whether they were actually Jewish or not.* The implication, echoing a perennial antisemitic canard, was that Jews preferred to benefit from war rather than fight in it. An open letter to a German Jew, published in the widely read *Harper's Weekly*, made these charges explicit: "You have no native, no political, no religious sympathy with this country," it declared. "You are here solely to make money, and your only wish is to make money as fast as possible."[9]

This image of the Jew carried over into the Union army, where, especially in the wake of Grant's order, some Jews found themselves persecuted and taunted. One of the highest-ranking Jews serving under Grant, Philip Trounstine, a captain in the Ohio Volunteer Cavalry, resigned from the army on account of the abuse that he was suffering. "Not alone my feelings, but the sense of Religious duty I owe to the religion of my Forefathers, were both deeply hurt and wounded in consequence of the late order of General Grant," he wrote his commanding officer, fully two months after that order had been revoked. "I can no longer bear the taunts and malice, of those to whom my religious opinions are known, brought on by the effect that, that order has instilled into their minds."[10]

The extent to which "Jews"—a tiny minority of about one half of one

---

* Civil War historian James M. McPherson observes that "harassed Union officers had come to use the word 'Jew' the same way many southerners used 'Yankee'—as a shorthand way of describing anyone they considered shrewd, acquisitive, aggressive, and possibly dishonest." *Battle Cry of Freedom: The Civil War Era* (New York: Oxford University Press, 1988), 622n61.

General William
Tecumseh Sherman

percent of the American population at that time—came to represent
malevolent forces harming the war effort as a whole is evident from the
more than one hundred references to Jews found in the subsequently published "Official Records" of the Union and Confederate armies, issued by
the Government Printing Office. In the months prior to Grant's order,
one finds Brigadier General Leonard F. Ross using "Jew owners" as a syn-
onym for "cotton speculators." Major General William Tecumseh Sherman warned officials in Washington (with a copy to General Grant) that
as a result of cotton trading in areas recaptured from the Confederacy,
"the country will swarm with dishonest Jews who will smuggle powder,
pistols, percussion-caps, &c." Major General William S. Rosecrans (himself often misidentified as a Jew) reported hearing that "large amounts
of goods, shipped by express from Louisville by Jews . . . have been sent
South." And Major General Benjamin F. Butler (who helped his brother
make a fortune in the illicit cotton trade) entreated Secretary of the Treasury Salmon P. Chase to prevent "the Jews from gathering up all the gold
in the country to exchange it with the Confederates for cotton."[11] While
some Jews, as we shall see, certainly did engage in smuggling and specu-

lating, these were actually common wartime practices profitably engaged in by Jews and non-Jews alike (including politicians and military men). The problem, which Jewish leaders like Isaac Leeser well understood, was that in the eyes of far too many people, these common practices had become perniciously identified with Jews alone.

This, however, was not the only cause for alarm in Jewish circles in the wake of Grant's order. The very term "Jews as a class" took Jews aback. Generally, the word "class" simply referred to individuals possessing common attributes, and used in that sense it was unobjectionable. When George Washington, in 1790, wrote to the Jews of Newport that he would always remember the cordial welcome he had received there "from all classes of citizens," nobody even noticed. When, a decade after the Civil War, North Carolina congressman Alfred Moore Waddell praised Jews "as a class" for being "orderly, industrious and intelligent members of society," nobody seems to have worried about that either. Indeed, references to a wide range of groups "as a class" abounded throughout the Civil War era. The "Official Records" of the war contain references to "negroes as a class," "Germans as a class," "Irish as a class," and "merchants as a class."[12]

Nevertheless, when Ulysses S. Grant accused "Jews as a class" of violating trade regulations and military orders, and ordered them expelled, that went beyond normative generalizations and group stereotypes. By indicting and punishing all Jews for the sins of just a few, Grant seemed to be hearkening back to an older, corporate view of the Jew common in the Middle Ages and lasting in many places well into modern times. "Jews as a class" meant that Jews were not treated as individuals, responsible for their own actions. Instead, Grant's order treated them as part of a Jewish collectivity, akin to the Jewish "nation" that the Dutch West India Company permitted to settle in New Amsterdam back in 1654, or to the Jews in the days of Jesus portrayed in Christian sermons and Sunday-school texts.

During the Civil War, to be sure, collective punishments were common; they were by no means confined to Jews alone. In Memphis, in 1862, General Sherman ordered that each time unarmed boats in the harbor were fired upon, "ten families must be expelled from Memphis." Their names were determined by lot, and they were given three days to move at least twenty-five miles from the city. A far more shocking example took place on August 25, 1863, when Brigadier General Thomas Ewing responded to a horrific Confederate massacre in Lawrence, Kansas, led by guerrilla leader William Clarke Quantrill, by expelling from their homes (most of which were subsequently looted and burned) "all persons" living in four rural Missouri counties. In so doing, he punished as many as twenty thousand people, including women and children, just because some of them had fed and sheltered the massacre's perpetrators. As fate would have it, that, too, was a "General Orders No. 11"—issued, of course, by Ewing—and Lincoln, in that terrible case, did not revoke it.[13]

The military in the Civil War (and long afterward) trained its officers to take quick and decisive measures based upon military considerations alone. Grant, in 1875, explained this to a visiting young rabbi looking to retrospectively understand his order expelling the Jews, but it was true of the Civil War as a whole: "Nice distinctions were disregarded. We had no time to handle things with kid gloves."[14] That remains an unfortunate characteristic of warfare. In World War II, Japanese Americans experienced even harsher forms of collective treatment, including banishment and internment, justified on the basis of individual malefactions and military necessity. Then, too, an entire group was deemed responsible for the misdeeds of individual members, and the misdeeds of individual members caused an entire group to suffer.

For Jews, meanwhile, Grant's order that they be "required to leave" the territory under his command, and that "any one returning . . . be arrested and held in confinement," inevitably called to mind memories, seared into the Jewish collective conscience, of expulsions from other lands where Jews had likewise considered themselves "at home"—until "required to leave." There was the great expulsion of Jews from England in 1290, and the expulsions from France in 1306 and 1394. Most of the major cities of Central Europe expelled the Jews during the four-teenth and fifteenth centuries—at least temporarily. The most cataclys-mic of all expulsions to its time—involving, some claim, well over one hundred thousand refugees—was the traumatic expulsion of Jews from Spain, in 1492, followed shortly thereafter by their expulsion from Por-tugal and from Naples. The Jews of Recife, in Brazil, were expelled in 1654 and the Jews of Prague in 1744. Thereafter, expulsions and threats of expulsion continued to hang over Jews' heads in many of the lands where they lived—threats that would be mercilessly carried out in the century following Grant's order, when more Jews were expelled from their homes in Europe and Arab lands than in all of previously recorded history put together. General Orders No. 11 echoed this doleful tradition. Its language sounded eerily familiar to Jews whose ancestors had been "required to leave" their homes many, many times before. But Jews never expected this to happen to them in America, dubbed by Francis Scott Key in 1814 "the land of the free and the home of the brave."[15]

Even less did they expect to be threatened with extermination, but that, too, happened in the wake of Grant's order, albeit from a journalist who allowed his prejudices to peek through his writing. On February 16, 1863, the Associated Press, described by its historian as "an authoritative source for news throughout the military conflict," reported the capture of three Jews found smuggling letters and medicines to New Orleans. The capture of wartime smugglers hardly made for sensational copy, so the reporter added some chilling thoughts of his own. "The Jews in New Orleans and all the South ought to be exterminated," he wrote. "They run the blockade, and are always found to be at the bottom of every new villainy." How many newspapers published this AP dispatch is unknown. Some actually editorialized against it. But its impact, coming on the heels of Grant's order, seems to have elicited a powerful emotional response from nervous Jews. "Must a class of citizens be condemned, decried, per-secuted, exterminated because some of them smuggle?" a visibly agitated

Isaac Mayer Wise wondered aloud. "Must we all suffer, we, our wives and our children, must we all be dishonored and disgraced, because three Jews were caught on a fishing smack loaded with contraband goods? With an aching heart and eyes filled with tears, the pen trembling between our fingers, we sit down to appeal to the World at large, to the holiness of humanity and the precepts of religion; in behalf of a defenceless minority, we appeal to all good men—for mercy's sake stop these outrages on thousands of innocent, industrious, loyal and honest persons; for our country's sake stop this disgracing condemnation of all on account of the few."[16]

Much as Jews agonized over antisemitism, expulsion, and even the muttered threat of extermination, the rhetoric of Isaac Leeser and Isaac Mayer Wise suggests that an uglier fear concerning the place of Jews in American society underlay some of their thinking as well. They worried, in the wake of the Emancipation Proclamation, that the status of Blacks would appreciably rise and the status of Jews correspondingly fall. Most slaves, after all, were Christian. If America no longer split along racial lines, might it cleave along religious lines, rendering Blacks insiders and Jews outsiders? Historians, understandably, have played down this fear, not wishing to besmirch the reputations of some of American Jewry's most illustrious leaders whose words, in retrospect, are painful to read.[17] But for a minority group with a long history of persecution, theirs was a natural fear. Experience had taught Jews to be eternally vigilant. Nor was the prejudice that Jewish leaders displayed in writing about Blacks at all uncommon in their day. In this respect, as in so much of their behavior surrounding the great issues of the Civil War, Jews simply resembled their white neighbors.

Isaac Mayer Wise, a fierce critic of abolitionists and their sometimes virulent anti-Jewish rhetoric, saw evidence of the declining status of Jews vis-à-vis Blacks in the way Congress debated Grant's order. The abolitionist leader William Lloyd Garrison, he knew, had once described the Jewish leader Mordecai Noah as "that lineal descendant of the monsters who nailed Jesus to the cross between two thieves." Abolitionist Edmund

Quincy of Boston likewise harbored fierce anti-Jewish sentiments. Now Wise wondered aloud whether Congressman Elihu Washburne, the Radical Republican who engineered the failure of the House of Representatives' censure resolution against Grant, likewise supported Blacks at Jews' expense. "If the Hebrew citizens of the United States were 'gentlemen of color,'" he sardonically suggested, "Mr. Washburne would certainly have made a brilliant effort to vindicate their rights and expose a general who committed a gross outrage on them. But being only white men, it would not pay."[18] Wise may have pretended here that Jews were simply a species of "white men," but he knew full well that Jews and non-Jews alike considered them to be a "class" apart. Many, indeed, considered Jews to be members of a distinctive "Jewish race."[19]

The *Jewish Record*, edited by Abraham S. Cohen of New York, in an open letter to Congress, echoed Wise's sentiments. "Supposing any general of the United States had issued an order expelling from his command all 'Negroes,'" the newspaper asked. "Would not 'sympathy for our oppressed brethren, without distinction of color,' have moved you to censure him?"[20]

These comments, at one level, pointed to the hypocrisy of those (like Washburne) who supported emancipation for Blacks while expressing contempt for Jews. Their sarcastic tone, though, indicates how much more was also at stake. Isaac Leeser's much longer discussion (written anonymously for the *Philadelphia Inquirer*, which refused to publish it, and printed instead in his own *Occident*) leaves little doubt that, at least to his mind, nothing less than the future status of the American Jew was on the line. He made this clear in the very title he gave to his piece—"Are Israelites Slaves?"—which, in the shadow of the Emancipation Proclamation, suggested that the ball and chain of victimization was being passed from one group to another. He then wondered aloud whether Jews fighting in the Civil War were sacrificing their lives "in a contest designed by those in authority to give freedom to the negro, only to bring expulsion from the Union territory to the descendants of the Hebrew race?" Finally, in perhaps the most outrageous and prejudiced paragraph that he ever wrote, Leeser proceeded to contrast the rising status of Black Americans with the forlorn condition of the country's Jews:

> Is there to be freedom for the colored races, who have never furnished a genius of towering intellect to the world, while we who have produced for Israel and all mankind the greatest of mortals, Moses the son of Amram, and for the Christians the founder of their faith . . . are even now to be ill-used and stigmatized for adhering to our faith? Why are tears shed for the sufferings of the African in his bondage, by which his moral condition has been immensely improved, in spite of all that may be alleged to the contrary, whereas for the Hebrews every one has words of contempt or acts of violence?[21]

Eastern Jews without familial ties to the South would not likely have written as Leeser did. Still, the fact that three different Jewish newspapers, including the two most important ones in the country (those of Leeser and Wise), contrasted the improving treatment of Blacks with the deteriorating treatment of Jews points to the grimness of Jewish fears. In the wake of Grant's order, the Emancipation Proclamation, and heightened antisemitic rhetoric nationwide, Jews worried that their starkest nightmares might actually come to pass.

Cooler heads understood perfectly well that smuggling and speculation formed the central basis for General Orders No. 11. The order specifically indicted Jews for "violating every regulation of trade," and complaints about Jews who traded "upon the miseries of the country" were legion.[22] Grant, determined to put down the South's rebellion and focused upon capturing Vicksburg, looked upon all smugglers as traitors. They gave aid and comfort to the enemy and prolonged the war. He favored a total embargo on trade with the South, complete with blockades and sieges.

Given the enormous pressures he was under to defeat the Southern rebels, he understandably lashed out at those who sought to undermine this strategy. He expelled the Jews to inhibit smuggling.

The fact that some Jews took advantage of wartime opportunities for smuggling is hardly surprising. All wars open up opportunities that enterprising individuals exploit. In the Civil War, the North (along with much of Europe) depended upon Southern cotton for clothes. "King Cotton," like Middle Eastern oil in our day, was a basic commodity; the textile industry on several continents relied upon it. As a result, when the supply of cotton declined, its price on the world market rose dramatically. Anyone with access to cotton could reap huge profits. Meanwhile, in the South, deepening shortages of goods once imported from the North, including medicine (especially quinine), bacon, salt, clothing, and shoes, drove prices of those necessities skyward. Bans on trading with the enemy, and the North's blockade of Southern ports, meant that these products had to be brought into the South illegally, at many times their original cost.

Such conditions—high demand, short supply—paved the way, as they always do, for canny traders and smugglers to profiteer; Rhett Butler, the fictional blockade-runner in *Gone With the Wind*, reflected that reality. At one point in the war, a bale (four hundred pounds) of cotton purchased in the South for $100 sold up north for $500, while four hundred pounds of bacon purchased in the North for $88 sold down south for $2,400 Confederate. An enterprising merchant who smuggled goods in both directions (and didn't get caught) could turn a $100 investment into a payoff of $2,000 or more. The risks involved were considerable, but the venturesome—Jews and non-Jews alike—found the temptation impossible to resist.[23]

Speculative opportunities multiplied once Union troops moved into the Mississippi Valley in 1862, capturing Nashville, New Orleans, and Memphis. President Lincoln insisted that trade should follow the flag, believing that improved economic circumstances in recaptured areas would promote loyalty to the Union. He also hoped to increase the supply of cotton available for export, so as to promote foreign exchange and dissuade foreign countries needing cotton from moving to the Confederacy's aid. In line with this policy, traders who swore oaths of allegiance to the United States received official government permits and even encouragement to trade local cotton for cash and dearly needed supplies. Predictably, these permits became much sought after; they offered a ticket to wealth. Equally predictably, Confederate loyalists soon found ways of exploiting the new trade policy to evade the Union blockade. They illicitly sold Southern cotton for gold, and then used the gold to obtain food, weapons, and supplies needed to stave off the Confederacy's defeat. Generals like Grant and Sherman were furious. Grant proposed that the government "buy all the Cotton at a fixed rate" and ship it north, thereby obviating the need for traders ("they are a curse to the Army") once and for all. Sherman agreed: "We cannot," he exclaimed, "carry on war and trade with a people at the same time." But traders—non-Jews and Jews, politicians and soldiers—took full advantage of the new trade regulations, which yielded handsome profits.[24]

Immigrant Jews were no strangers to smuggling and illicit transactions of these sorts. As peddlers and traders, numbers of them possessed the skills, the connections, the temperament, and the nerves that such activities required. Some probably knew Jews who engaged in cross-border smuggling in Europe. For generations, the economic restrictions and confiscatory taxes that weighed heavily upon Jews in Central and Eastern Europe encouraged illicit means of gain. In 1820, the organized Jewish community of Vilna placed a ban on smuggling from neighboring Austrian and Prussian provinces into Russia—a sure sign that the practice was common. In Warsaw, well over 80 percent of all those caught smuggling goods between 1842 and 1849 were Jews (perhaps because officials turned a blind eye toward non-Jewish smugglers). Smuggling, in some of these cases, was a form of rebellion against rules deemed unjust. The fact that smuggling also proved extraordinarily lucrative only added to its appeal.[25]

How many of America's 150,000 or so Jews smuggled in violation of trade regulations during the Civil War is impossible to know. Some unquestionably did, whereas "Jews as a class" unquestionably did not. Cincinnati's Mount Carmel Lodge of the Jewish fraternal order B'nai B'rith communicated a private warning on this subject:

> Information has been received here, doubtless authentic, proving the fact of certain of our co-religionists being engaged in an illegal traffic and other acts of disloyalty with those who are in rebellion against the Government. . . . We fraternally call your attention to this subject, urging your vigilance to suppress all acts of disloyalty, especially among those who style themselves members of the B'nai B'rith.[26]

A few Jews, in the post–Civil War years, produced elaborate accounts of their smuggling adventures. Heyman Herzberg, in Atlanta, joined "a couple of men who had already made money as blockade-runners and were preparing to go north once more." He blundered, was arrested, and his goods were taken from him. While he did eventually make it to Philadelphia for a reunion with his family, he arrived a good deal poorer than he had left. Undaunted, he prepared to smuggle goods in the other direction, heeding advice from his brothers, who told him that "they ran the blockade by way of Memphis and got through without trouble." Once again, he miscalculated, but he did manage to smuggle some goods through the lines to the South. He did not reveal how much money he made selling them, but his account serves as a further reminder that smuggling was a risky business, fraught with dangers.[27]

Aaron Hirsch of Batesville, Arkansas, proved much more successful. His tale of passing through military lines to trade cotton for gold and

Memphis, Tennessee: hauling sugar and cotton from
their hiding places for shipment north, 1862

quinine in Memphis, in addition to its comfort with slavery, explains why
generals like Grant and Sherman were so disgusted by the administration's policy, and so angry at smugglers and those who abetted them:

> Medicine was very much needed, and having none, I took a few bales
> of cotton, secured permission to pass the Confederate lines, went by
> land some 120 miles with my negroes, sold the cotton in Memphis,
> receiving for same quinine and gold. Coming back into Arkansas, I
> had to pass the [Mississippi] River, which was a great risk because
> both gold and quinine was strictly forbidden to be brought into the
> Confederate lines. I then discovered that an old carpenter and wife,
> who formerly worked for me, were living in Memphis. I got his wife
> to make an old flannel undershirt for my negro and sewed all the
> gold I had in this shirt. It was two or three days before I obtained
> a pass to leave, and during this time my negro was walking around

town with this money on his person. He was then as free a man as I, being in Memphis, but he was faithful to me and got through the lines all right.[28]

The most appalling account of Jewish smuggling in and around Memphis was produced by an eyewitness, the ardent secessionist Abraham E. Frankland, whose family numbered among the earliest Jewish settlers in the state. Preserved in manuscript and published only in 1957, the *Kronikals*, written in pseudo-biblical language, paints a devastating portrait of the merchants who descended upon Memphis following its capture and confirms that "the most of them were of the descendants of Israel . . . Israelites of Cincinnati." Memphis's Rabbi Simon Tuska, so Frankland recalled, appealed to these Northern traders to leave:

> Why must you ever entail prejudices upon yourselves by bringing to bear the envy and contempt of the nations of the earth. Have ye not suffered sufficiently? Must ye also be driven out of this land by the Gentiles, who may become infuriated against thee?

Yet instead of heeding the rabbi's advice, the Jewish merchants, seeking "to grow fat and rich upon the necessities of those that had sojourned here," set themselves up in commerce. Memphis Jews neither associated with them, "nor did they invite them to thier [*sic*] habitations, nor hold friendly intercourse with them," Frankland admiringly wrote, for the Jewish merchants from the North took the oath in fealty to the Union and the local Jewish merchants refused. Before long, though, "foreigners" began to purchase cotton "with virgin gold." "Speculators went from house to house . . . cotton!, cotton!, cotton!" Local Jewish businessmen, who needed the money, joined them in these speculations and "had the same conveyed in large arks to the great . . . City of New York." Both "foreign" and "local" merchants thus engaged in risky and illicit activities, according to Frankland's caustic recollections. "Were the historian to recite the many and various schemes perfected during the war by the merchant princes, they would seem herculaneon [*sic*]," he concluded. "But the writer is satisfied that the schemes of our So[u]thern princes were as nought compared with the stupendous and gigantic ones of the people of the North."[29]*

Non-Jewish accounts of Memphis confirm many of Frankland's assertions. "The Israelites have come down upon the city like locusts," a Chicago *Times* reporter wrote in July 1862. "Anything in the line of trade . . . may be obtained of these eager gentlemen at ruinous prices." Another account recalled that "the long dining-hall of the principal hotel at Memphis, looked at meal-times like a Feast of the Passover." A later account, from Assistant Secretary of War Charles A. Dana (who himself secretly speculated in cotton), complained of a "mania for sudden fortunes made in cotton, raging in a vast population of Jews and Yankees." Dana uncovered widespread corruption among soldiers eager to share in the profits that illicit trading by civilians yielded. "Every colonel, captain, or quar-

---

* These schemes sometimes made it difficult to distinguish between honest and dishonest forms of trade. On January 25, 1864, for example, the schooner *Thomas F. Dawson*, on its way from Richmond to Baltimore, was captured by a Union armed transport. It was found to contain tobacco, jewelry, gold, silver, bonds, and banknotes in the possession of five Jews named Philip Epstein, M. David, Henry Steen, Julius Louis, and Herman Sommers, who were discovered hidden in the hold of the vessel. The five Jews were jailed and the government seized their effects as contraband and sold them for $16,703 (more than $226,000 in today's money). Subsequently, however, the Jews appealed to the secretary of war, insisting that they had only been "availing themselves of the advantages of the . . . amnesty proclamation" issued by President Lincoln. They argued that since they were fleeing "rebel tyranny," they should have been allowed to proceed freely. The men sought compensation for the money and property seized from them and demanded "substantial justice" for wrongful imprisonment and ill treatment. General Benjamin F. Butler, who distrusted Jews, scornfully dismissed their claims, but some in Congress proved more sympathetic. The House of Representatives collected documents in the case, filling some fifty closely printed pages. Ultimately, the secretary of war endorsed Butler's findings. The documents in the case, as a result, were "laid on the table and ordered to be printed." House of Representatives, *Letter from the Secretary of War in Answer to a Resolution of the House of the 5th Instant Transmitting All the Papers and Testimony Relating to the Claim of Philip Epstein and Others*, 39th Congress, 1st Session, Ex Doc. No. 9 (1865).

termaster is in secret partnership with some operator in cotton; every soldier dreams of adding a bale of cotton to his monthly pay." Instead of blaming Jews alone, Dana portrayed a whole culture of corruption involving traders and soldiers, Jews and non-Jews alike. "The amount of plunder & bribery that is going on in and about the City of Memphis is beyond all calculation," the city's commanding general agreed. "Soldiers on picket are bribed, officers are bribed. . . . Honesty is the exception and peculation [embezzlement] the rule wherever the army is brought into contact with trade."[30]

Ulysses S. Grant had long been concerned about traders, speculators, and smugglers in his territory. Immigrant Jews, who looked, dressed, and sounded distinctive particularly caught his attention. They cared only about their own fortunes, he thought, while he worried about the fortunes of the Union as a whole. He also worried that traders who slipped over into the Confederacy would pass along classified military information that they had gleaned along the way, such as where troops were camped and where they were headed (traders who passed from the Confederacy to the North, he knew, did the same).[31] Grant, given his aims, believed in employing economic warfare alongside military actions against the South; this greatly contributed to his success, especially at Vicksburg. To his mind, any trade with the South, legal or illegal, inevitably hindered the war effort. He did whatever he could to limit it.[32]

As early as July 1862, Grant ordered the commander of the District of the Mississippi to "examine all baggage of all speculators coming South," and to turn back those who were carrying gold ("specie"). "Jews," he admonished, "should receive special attention." In August, a soldiers' newspaper quoted Grant as calling Jews "a nuisance." It intimated that he had plans to "abate" that nuisance. Nothing happened for several months, but on November 9, as he prepared to move south in preparation for the decisive battle at Vicksburg, Grant tightened his regulations against Jews: "Refuse all permits to come south of Jackson for the present," he ordered. "The Isrealites [*sic*] especially should be kept out." The very next day he strengthened that order: "No Jews are to be permitted to travel on the Rail Road southward from any point . . . they are such an intolerable nuisance that the Department must be purged for [*sic*] them." Writing in early December to General Sherman, whose quartermaster had created problems by selling cotton "to a Jew by the name of Haas," Grant explained that "in consequence of the total disregard and evasion of orders by the Jews my policy is to exclude them so far as practicable from the Dept."[33]

Nevertheless, when Colonel John Van Deusen Du Bois on December 8, 1862, angrily ordered "All Cotton-Speculators, Jews and other Vagrants having no honest means of support, except trading upon the miseries of their Country" to leave Holly Springs and gave them "twenty-four hours or they will be sent to duty in the trenches," Grant insisted that the draconian order be rescinded. "Instructions from Washington," he reminded Du Bois, "are to encourage getting Cotton out of the country." Regardless of his private opinions and actions, Grant understood that he still had to publicly uphold official government policy, which permitted those loyal to the Union to trade in cotton.[34]

Why then did Grant himself expel "Jews as a class" from the entire territory under his command just nine days later? Clearly, and notwithstanding subsequent claims to the contrary, the order fit into a pattern of orders that he had issued over many months. Grant identified a widespread practice—smuggling—with a visible group and blamed "Jews as a class" for what was in fact an inevitable by-product of wartime shortages exploited by Jews and non-Jews, civilians and military men alike. But if that was the cause, the occasion for the order remains somewhat mysterious, especially since Grant had so recently countermanded a more limited order expelling Jews. Three different explanations have been proposed.

Multiple sources have always maintained that Grant acted in response to instructions from Washington. Supposedly, he received a telegram from officials there warning that Jews were buying up gold "to take to the South to invest in cotton." The purported telegram gave him clear instructions: "Issue an order expelling from your lines all Jews who can not give satisfactory evidence of their honesty of intentions." An informant with the ominous nom de guerre of "Gentile" reported in the *Cincinnati Commercial* that he was sitting with Grant when this telegram arrived. Grant's father, Jesse R. Grant, insisted that his son's order "was issued on express instructions from Washington." Even Isaac Mayer Wise, no supporter of Grant, found the report credible: "It appears a fact that Gen. Grant received instruction from Washington to drive the Jewish traders out of his line . . . it must have come from the Treasury Department." Diligent searches, however, have failed to turn up any such telegram, even though government records from the Civil War are extraordinarily complete. As we shall see, Edward Rosewater, the Jewish editor of the *Omaha Bee* and a telegraph officer in the White House when General Orders No. 11 was issued, testified years later that "only three men in Washington had authority to issue orders to Gen. Grant," and none of them ordered him to expel the Jews. Moreover, even the purported telegram that Grant received made no mention of expelling "Jews as a class." Had Grant simply expelled those Jews who could not give "satisfactory evidence of their honesty of intentions," the response to his order would likely have been altogether different.[35]

A second explanation suggests that military personnel wanted Jews out of the way so that they themselves could monopolize the cotton trade. Jewish traders unquestionably competed with soldiers to purchase Southern cotton, and often outbid them. Indeed, no sooner were the Jews expelled than the purchase price of cotton fell from forty cents a pound to twenty-five cents a pound—a boon to speculators who already enjoyed outsize profits on sales of the staple in the North. Cincinnati newspapers cleverly transformed this effect of the expulsion into its cause ("the Jews must leave, because they interfere with a branch of military business"), but the claim does not bear close scrutiny. Grant himself never traded in cotton, and on the very day that he expelled the Jews he called for the government "to buy all the Cotton at a fixed rate" and send it north for

Jesse R. Grant

sale, a plan that would have ended military and civilian trade in the commodity altogether. Corrupt soldiers may indeed have wanted Jews out of
the way, but there is no evidence that Grant was acting on their behalf.[36]

The third and most likely reason for the timing of Grant's order
concerns a visit in mid-December from his sixty-eight-year-old father,
accompanied by members of the prominent Mack family of Cincinnati,
significant Jewish clothing manufacturers. Harman, Henry, and Simon
Mack, as part of an ingenious scheme, had formed a secret partnership
with the ever-entrepreneurial and somewhat shady elder Grant. In return
for 25 percent of their profits, he agreed to accompany them to his son's
Mississippi headquarters, act as their agent to "procure a permit for them
to purchase cotton," and help them secure the means to transport the
cotton to New York. The Macks surely did not know how troubled the
relationship between Ulysses S. Grant and his father was: Ulysses, like
many a child who sets off on his own path, craved his father's approval
but winced at many of the old man's shortcomings. In this case, according to journalist Sylvanus Cadwallader, an eyewitness, the younger Grant
waxed indignant at his father's crass attempt to profit from his military
status, and raged at the Jewish traders who "entrapped his old father into

Julia Dent Grant

such an unworthy undertaking." He refused to provide the permit, sent the Macks homeward "on the first train for the north," and in high dudgeon immediately issued the order expelling "Jews as a class" from his territory. Jesse R. Grant's involvement in this scheme provides "a psychological explanation" for General Orders No. 11, according to John Simon, the scholarly editor of *The Papers of Ulysses S. Grant.* In a classic act of displacement, the general "expelled the Jews rather than his father."[37]

Ulysses S. Grant himself never made public mention of his father's corrupt scheme with the Macks. Nor, in 1863, did he provide any other justification for General Orders No. 11. He accepted Lincoln's revocation of the order in silence and offered no defense of his actions before Congress. In his long and justly celebrated *Personal Memoirs,* written just prior to his death, he also made no mention of General Orders No. 11. "That was a matter long past and best not referred to," his son Frederick quoted him as saying when he pointed out the omission to him. Just as the memoirs passed over in silence other embarrassing episodes from the war, most notably the general's bouts of drunkenness, so, too, did they ignore his order expelling "Jews as a class."[38]

Julia Dent Grant, the memoir writer's high-spirited wife, proved far less circumspect. In her own memoirs, written following her husband's death and published only in 1975, she went out of her way to mention Grant's order "expelling the Jews from his lines," characterizing it as nothing less than "obnoxious." The general, she recalled, felt that the severe reprimand he received for the order was deserved, for "he had no right to make an order against any special sect."[39]

Had Ulysses S. Grant expressed such sentiments himself back in 1863, the subsequent course of his relationship with the Jewish community might have been altogether different. As it was, he found himself compared, in some Jewish circles, to historic enemies of the Jewish people, a long and ignoble list. The most common comparison was to the wicked Haman, vizier of Persia and villain of the biblical book of Esther, whose order to exterminate the Jews of his day was overturned by Persia's King Ahasuerus—with disastrous consequences for Haman and his family. The Hebrew journal *Hamagid*, published in the Prussian town of Lyck, in recounting the Grant episode for Hebrew-speaking Jews across Europe, used the very language of the book of Esther to underscore these parallels between the biblical story and the contemporary one. It also anticipated that Jews would one day have their revenge on the general: "The day will come," it predicted, "when he will pay in judgment for all of the damage that he wrought upon the Children of Israel by his ignorant and wicked order, and his deeds will recoil upon his own head."[40]

3

The Election of 1868

The man who might have been expected to lead the Jewish community's revenge upon Ulysses S. Grant was a young, self-assured lawyer named Simon Wolf.[1] Born in the tiny town of Hinzweiler in Germany's Rhenish provinces, Wolf portrayed himself as one of those immigrants who fell in love with America even before immigrating there. An American uncle had sent him a picture of George Washington and a copy of the Declaration of Independence when he was nine years old and, according to the account he published seventy years later, he was instantly smitten. "What a wonderful man George Washington must have been," he recalled thinking, "and what a fairyland it must be, where all men are born free and equal." By the time he himself arrived in the United States, on July 19, 1848, in the company of his grandparents, he felt himself to be "to all intents and purposes an American."[2]

Wolf spent his adolescence in Uhrichsville, Ohio, a rural town chiefly remembered for being about a hundred miles equidistant from Cleveland, Columbus, and Pittsburgh. There his uncle, like so many Jewish peddlers who accumulated capital, had settled down and opened a general store. Wolf served as his uncle's clerk, ran the store himself for four years, fell in love with politics, and eventually determined to study law. Like many another aspiring Midwest lawyer at that time, he read law in the offices of a local judge, took a course of lectures, and was admitted to the bar following what he recalled as a perfunctory oral examination.

Uhrichsville could not long contain a man of Wolf's ambitions. "Depen-

Simon Wolf

dence upon local practice here for an attorney meant starvation," one community historian recalled.[3] The rapid expansion of government during the Civil War suggested that far more plentiful opportunities—for remunerative work and for political influence—would be found in Washington, D.C. Wolf moved there in 1862, just six months before Grant issued General Orders No. 11.

Building upon his intimate ties to the fraternal network of B'nai B'rith members, Wolf quickly found work in the nation's capital advocating for Southern Jews arrested while trying to pass through military lines to find refuge in the North. On one occasion, he also successfully intervened with Abraham Lincoln to save the life of a Jewish serviceman sentenced to be shot for desertion. "Mr. President," he recalled pleading, "what would you have done under similar circumstances? If your dying mother had summoned you to her bedside to receive her last message before her soul would be summoned to its Maker, would you have been a deserter to her who gave you birth rather than a deserter in law but not in fact to the flag to which you had sworn allegiance?" The unwavering courage, florid oratory, and passionate emotion that Wolf displayed in his successful bid to save the soldier's life served him well in Washington. He quickly rose to become the Jewish community's premier unofficial government lobbyist. Combining traditional behind-the-scenes defenses of his people, characteristic of the European court Jew, or *shtadlan*, with more modern advocacy tools, such as public speeches and frequent appearances in the press, he curried favor with those in power, interceded vigorously on Jews' behalf, dropped names shamelessly, and, as time went on, reveled in his own self-importance. Tellingly, he entitled his autobiography *The Presidents I Have Known*.[4]

Wolf played a minor role in 1862, when General Orders No. 11 was issued. Though he later recalled that he "heartily cooperated" in the whole affair, his principal contribution as an ambitious twenty-six-year-old consisted of an able letter to the editor entitled "Defence of the Jews" that he published in the *Washington Chronicle*. Insisting that Jews were as devoted to the Union and to the war "as any other sect or nation," he pointed to their manifold contributions to the war effort, condemned Grant's order as an evil precedent, and promised that history would vindicate Jews, for, as he put it, "the dark ages have passed."[5]

Wolf may momentarily have questioned that judgment when he himself was arrested during the war, on the grounds that he associated with B'nai B'rith, alleged to be a "disloyal organization" that was "helping the traitors." The charges reveal more about the spirit of the times than about B'nai B'rith. Those responsible for domestic security during the Civil War, like their more recent counterparts, cast suspicion on legions of innocent people, immigrants in particular. Fortunately for Wolf, Secretary of War Edwin Stanton characterized the arrest as an outrage and personally intervened to free him.[6]

Wolf's first years in Washington coincided with Ulysses S. Grant's ascent to greatness. The general's successes at Vicksburg and Chattanooga, his promotion to major general and then lieutenant general, and, finally, his acceptance of Robert E. Lee's surrender on April 9, 1865, at Appomattox Court House transformed Grant into a national hero. His picture adorned patriotic posters, his exploits were widely reported, and many felt that he was destined, someday, to be president of the United States. In the meanwhile, following the assassination of Abraham Lincoln, Grant moved with his family to Washington and in 1866 was elevated to a new rank, higher even than that held by George Washington back in the American Revolution. He was appointed general of the armies of the United States.[7]

Wolf, making his way in the city, had ample opportunity to observe Grant in his new roles. He was particularly impressed by him, he later recalled, when he watched him in action at the Grand Review (May 23–24, 1865), where Union armies marched through Washington in triumphant celebration of their victory over the Confederacy. "Grant on that day represented in his outward demeanor an absolute repose," he recollected, perhaps seeking to explain his changing views of the man. "There was no vindictiveness in his face; the fires that lighted up his eyes were not those of grim satisfaction at being the conqueror, but rather those of a man who was pleased to know that the country was once more united and that the war, with all its horrors, had ceased."[8]

It soon became clear to Wolf, as well as to others who contemplated the political landscape, that Grant "would unquestionably be the candidate of the Republican party for President of the United States."[9] This posed an unprecedented and deeply vexing dilemma for Jews. Could they vote for a man—even a national hero—who once had expelled "Jews as a class" from his war zone? If not, would this set Jews apart from the multitudes who viewed Grant as the savior of his country? Worse yet, might it raise the ugly specter of dual loyalty, suggesting that Jews cared more about "Jewish issues," such as antisemitism, than about the welfare of the country as a whole?

Concern about "factional politics," of course, dated all the way back to the beginning of the republic. Appeals to different voting blocs, as well as outrage at such craven appeals, characterized some of America's earliest elections. Long before political polling became a science, pundits speculated about the voting habits of different ethnic and religious groups. In 1841, the earliest known analysis of the Jewish vote in New York reported that "most of the Portuguese Jews are Whigs; of the German Jews, about half are Whigs; of the Pollakim [Polish Jews] about one-third," an indication that wealthier Jews had, at that time, come to support the more conservative Whig Party. Catholic voters, in 1844, faced a crisis when the Whig Party nominated the staunchly anti-Catholic Theodore Frelinghuysen as vice president on the ticket with Henry Clay (whom New York's Catholic archbishop, John Hughes, was otherwise known to admire). James Polk won that election by a razor-thin margin. Whether the Catholic vote swayed the scales remains a matter of conjecture.[10]

Jews, however, had not faced this problem before in a presidential election. Antisemitic charges had marred some presidential campaigns, notably the tempestuous campaign of 1800 when local Federalists desperately tarred their opponents as "vermin of foreign countries" and "Jews." Yet nobody imagined that the major party candidates in that election—John Adams and Thomas Jefferson—were themselves enemies of the Jewish people.[11] In Grant's case, by contrast, the candidate himself *was* the issue. Much of the country loved him, while a great many Jews found it hard to forgive him.

Simon Wolf alluded to this problem in a March 1868 address memorializing Isaac Leeser, the recently deceased Jewish leader and editor of *The Occident*. Just a few weeks had passed since Grant had publicly broken with President Andrew Johnson over the "Tenure of Office" act that Congress had passed to limit the president's power to hire and fire cabinet members. Bowing to congressional demands, Grant had allowed Edwin Stanton to resume his position as secretary of war, leading Johnson to charge his general in chief with betrayal. The public spat fueled speculation that the Republican Party would now nominate Grant for president of the United States. Against this background, Wolf, himself a Republican of stature, recalled that Leeser "was deeply pained that his fellow citizens . . . bore patiently the infamous order of a celebrated general which banished free American citizens from loyal ground." With talk of Grant's nomination probably uppermost in his thoughts, he reminded his listeners that "nothing that transpired during the war caused more indignation or deserves more lasting execration" than General Orders No. 11.[12]

Isaac Mayer Wise, a dyed-in-the-wool Democrat, was characteristically more blunt in addressing Grant's candidacy. "In case of his nomination to the presidency, which we hope will not take place," he wrote just a few days prior to Wolf's address, "we will consider it our duty to oppose him and the party nominating him. . . . Worse than General Grant none in this nineteenth century in civilized countries has abused and outraged the Jews."[13]

Several Democratic newspapers, eager to advance their party's humbled political fortunes, reprinted Wise's words or took their cue from him. They understood that for the Democrats to be victorious over a national hero like Grant, they would need to undermine his commanding public image. General Orders No. 11—scarcely known to most Americans in 1868 and shocking in its language and tone—served that purpose well. As a result, even newspapers in communities with barely any Jews pointed to the order as part of their examination of the presumed candidate's record. The *Flemingsburg Democrat* of Flemingsburg, Kentucky, for example, devoted two full columns in its issue of March 6, 1868, to "Gen. Grant and the Jews." The paper reprinted verbatim his order expelling the Jews and observed that "no order issued during the late war, was less called for, or more wantonly wrong." It assured local residents, whose knowledge of Jews largely came from the Bible, that "the Jews, as a class, are the most industrious and peaceable people we have among us." And it contrasted the persecution of the Jews by "the brutal soldier" (Grant) with the more positive treatment accorded them by military heroes like England's Oliver Cromwell, credited with securing the readmission of Jews into England. "History mentioned many wrongs inflicted on [Jews] in earlier times," the paper concluded, "but none more outrageous than this of the nineteenth century."[14]

The *New York World*, a Democratic newspaper, likewise printed reports on Grant's order once his candidacy for the Republican nomination seemed assured, as did newspapers in Memphis (under the headline "Grant's Brutality Towards the Jews") and Savannah, all cities with significant Jewish populations. The *St. Louis Dispatch*, meanwhile, published what it claimed to be an additional anti-Jewish remark by Grant, from a note he sent to President Lincoln after General Orders No. 11 was revoked. "In obedience to your instructions," it purportedly read, "the order complained of shall be recalled; but I take the liberty of saying that these people complained of are the same who crucified our Savior, and from the specimens of them here, I do not think the race has improved any since then." In fact, no such letter has ever been found, nor was Grant corresponding directly with Lincoln at that time. While the *Dispatch* credited "several citizens of St. Louis" for the story, and they supposedly heard it directly from Lincoln's lips, the story is almost certainly apocryphal. Still, the quote was memorable and the report impossible to disprove. As a consequence, the tale circulated widely.[15]

The impeachment trial of Andrew Johnson soon distracted the country, edging Grant's bid for the presidency from the headlines. There were no primaries in those days (the first preceded the presidential election of 1912), so the decision would be up to the Republican convention, meeting in May. In the meanwhile, Grant wisely laid low. While others soiled their reputations through the grueling impeachment trial, which ended in acquittal, "Ulysses the Silent" kept his mouth shut and bided his time.[16]

By late spring, Grant's nomination seemed inevitable. "The convention is about to assemble," he explained to his wife, "and, from all I hear, they will nominate me; and I suppose if I am nominated, I will be elected." War veterans, meeting in Chicago in May, all but demanded that he be selected the Republican nominee. Even old Jesse Grant spoke up in his son's support. A note of suspense was sounded when it was suggested that Ulysses might decline the honor, but few believed that. Finally, on May 21, General John A. Logan officially placed Grant's name in nomination. The floor of the Republican convention immediately erupted into one of the well-planned "spontaneous" demonstrations for which American political conventions are justly famed. By the time the tumult died down, the nomination was Grant's—unanimously and on the first ballot. Subsequently, a more divided convention nominated the Speaker of the House, Schuyler Colfax of Indiana, to be his running mate.[17]*

Following custom, Grant made no personal appearance at the convention. He only learned of his nomination while sitting at his desk in Washington when Edwin Stanton rushed in with a telegram. When Republican leaders visited him at his Washington home on May 29, he accepted the nomination, presumably with a ritualistic display of humble resignation. His handwritten letter of acceptance, dated that same day, provided Americans with a wise and pithy statement of his maturing political views:

> If elected to the office of the President of the United States, it will be my endeavor to administer all the laws in good faith, with economy, and with the view of giving peace, quiet, and protection everywhere. In times like the present it is impossible, or at least eminently improper, to lay down a policy to be adhered to, right or wrong, through an administration of four years. New political issues, not foreseen, are constantly arising; the views of the public on old ones are constantly changing, and a purely administrative officer should always be left free to execute the will of the people. I always have respected that will, and always shall.
>
> Peace and universal prosperity, its sequence, with economy of

---

* Colfax, back in 1859, had complained "of the omission to include Jewish ministers in the list of those who offer prayers in turn at the opening of Congress." He was chiefly responsible for the fact that on February 1, 1860, Rabbi Morris J. Raphall became the first rabbi ever to perform that religious function, praying with his head covered and attired in a traditional prayer shawl. This, however, seems to have been completely forgotten by 1868; it went unmentioned in the campaign. Bertram W. Korn, *Eventful Years and Experiences: Studies in Nineteenth Century American Jewish History* (Cincinnati: American Jewish Archives, 1954), 110–12.

administration, will lighten the burden of taxation, while it constantly reduces the national debt.

The concluding four words of this characteristically brief and to-the-point letter effectively captured the mood of the country and became Grant's campaign slogan, rallying cry, and, later, the four words printed above his tomb: "Let us have peace."[18]

The question, for Jews, was peace at what price? Should they insist on an explanation or an apology from Grant? Or should they join hands with Grant's Democratic opponents and turn General Orders No. 11 into a campaign issue? Back in 1863, it was easy for angry Jews to dream of the vengeance they might wreak against their oppressor, turning the tables on him much as their biblical ancestors had done to that archetypal anti-Jewish schemer Haman, the vizier of Persia. Such dreams still came easily to Jews living in or near the old Confederacy, who hated the "Unclean, Stinking Generallissimo" with a passion.[19] But now this "Haman" was a hero to many of his former soldiers and countrymen, and a candidate for the presidency of the United States. Was revenge still in order? Or might Ulysses S. Grant somehow be cleansed of the stain of antisemitism and rehabilitated?*

A pamphlet entitled *General Grant and the Jews*, published in New York City soon after Grant's nomination, made the case for revenge. Its pseudonymous author, Ph. von Bort, denounced Grant for issuing General Orders No. 11 and described him as unfit for the presidency. "As a CLASS, you have stigmatized and expelled us!" it declared, as if speaking in the name of every Jew. "As a CLASS, we rise up and vote against you, like one man!" The pamphlet ("in the name of all American Jews")

---

* Cesar Kaskel, based on his role in overturning General Orders No. 11, might have been expected to play a major part in this debate, but he seems instead to have remained completely silent. Having opened an upscale New York clothing store at Broadway and Bleecker Street in 1867, he likely concluded that any public political involvement on his part would have been bad for business.

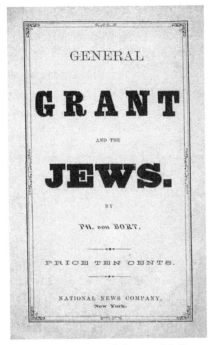

General Grant and the Jews (1868)

concluded with a bold and almost unprecedented statement of Jewish power—remarkable for what it reveals about American Jewry's confident optimism in 1868, but discomforting seeing how antisemites would later turn such characterizations back against Jews and accuse them of controlling the destinies of nations. "We are numerous," the pamphlet warned, "we are influential, we are wealthy, we are diffused over the whole continent, we are as one family; wherever our influence reaches, every Jew—no matter of what political party—every Jew, with the votes he can command, will endeavor to defeat, and with God's blessing, *will* defeat you!"[20]

The stakes were high. The Democratic Party had been gaining power in local and state elections during the last year of Andrew Johnson's presidency. Even Grant's hometown of Galena, Illinois, had elected a

Democratic mayor. So a close national election was forecast. A Jewish community of 150,000 to 200,000, many of them women, minors, or otherwise ineligible to vote as recent immigrants, might not appear to have been of great political significance. But Americans have regularly exaggerated the size and political power of the Jewish community—even back in 1868. Besides, in tight elections, as the nation periodically rediscovers, every vote counts.[21]

Party differences appeared particularly consequential in 1868, for in the balance hung the fate of four million freedmen, underprivileged former slaves who had benefited politically, socially, and economically from the Reconstruction-era policies that Republicans championed. The opposition Democrats, firmly aligned with the white race, promised sharp policy changes "to rescue the country from the anarchy of Radicalism." Their goal was to disenfranchise and disempower "the ruling horde of illiterate and brutal negro suffragans." "The Negro," one Democratic Party banner read, "May Become a Republican, a Slave, or a Tyrant!; but Never a Democrat."[22]

Against this background, liberal-minded Jews who disagreed with the pseudonymous pamphleteer of *General Grant and the Jews* and supported the Republican Party got busy. Lewis N. Dembitz, a noted Louisville attorney and scholar who courageously opposed slavery and was an early supporter of Abraham Lincoln (as well as the uncle and idol of future Supreme Court justice Louis Dembitz Brandeis) sent a letter of inquiry concerning General Orders No. 11 to Grant's headquarters. He received a long, courteous reply, clearly intended for distribution, from John A. Rawlins, who had cosigned the order as Grant's assistant adjutant general back in 1862 and now served as one of his prime advisers and spokesmen. Rawlins candidly recalled the violations "by persons principally of the Jewish race" that led up to the order. He explained why Grant decided "whether wisely or unwisely" to issue the order. Finally, with an eye toward the coming election, he told Dembitz what he and other Jewish Republicans desperately wanted to hear: allegations that the order "was issued on account of the religion of the Jews cannot be seriously entertained by any one who knows the General's steadfast adherence to the principles of American liberty and religious toleration."[23]

Simon Wolf likewise got busy. Notwithstanding his earlier suggestion that Grant's order merited "lasting execration," he now shifted from dreams of revenge to endeavors at rehabilitation. His long-standing devotion to the Republican Party and its policies, the favorable personal impression that Grant made upon him, and, likely as not, his own political ambitions led Wolf to try to clear the air on Grant's behalf. Even before the general's official nomination, Wolf addressed him on the subject of his order, subtly suggesting how it might be explained away. Grant, as usual, did not reply; he considered stony silence the best remedy for awkward problems. But Adam Badeau, his former military secretary who now handled his political correspondence, replied on Grant's behalf. Echoing the very language that Wolf had proposed, he wrote:

> General Grant . . . instructs me to say that the order was, as you suppose, "directed simply against evil designing persons whose religion was in no way material to the issue." When it was made, the guilty parties happened to be Israelites, exclusively; and it was intended to reach the guilty parties, not to wound the feelings of any others. It would have been made just as stringent against any other class of individuals, religious, political or commercial.[24]

Satisfied by this response, Wolf transformed himself into a tireless campaigner on Grant's behalf, "making speeches in different parts of the country, notably the crucial states of Ohio and Indiana." He became the first Washington Jewish leader to declare Grant rehabilitated, persuading himself, against all evidence, that Grant's order "never harmed anyone" and that Grant "had absolutely nothing to do with the said order." In time, he became a friend and loyal acolyte of the general's—so much so that he named his son, born in 1869, Adolph Grant Wolf.[25]

In a different way, the Seligman brothers, merchants and bankers, also got busy. Jesse and Henry Seligman, immigrants from Bavaria, had first met Grant back in 1848 when he entered their dry goods store in Watertown, New York, to buy "a bit of finery for his bride of a few months." The brothers were about the same age as Grant, and they all became fast friends. This friendship eventually expanded to embrace the eleven brothers and sisters of the Seligman clan, led by elder brother Joseph. During the Civil War, the Seligmans strongly supported the Union cause and the Republican Party. They helped to outfit New York's Seventh Regiment, marketed U.S. government war bonds in Europe, and received lucrative military contracts for uniforms and accessories. They were unaffected by General Orders No. 11, and their response to it is unknown. But in 1868, they contributed generously to Grant's campaign. Henry Seligman, then in Germany, predicted that Grant would "walk over and beat the [Democratic] party and its standard bearers" and that "all intelligent portions of our race" would keep religion out of the contest. Brothers Joseph, James, and Jesse, according to a history of the House of Seligman, "threw themselves wholeheartedly into the campaign to elect their friend." Abraham Seligman, from his base in San Francisco, likewise aided Grant. How much the family collectively contributed to the campaign's coffers cannot be known, but it was enough to secure banker Joseph Seligman a spot directly behind Grant at the inauguration.[26]

The majority of American Jews, however, were not nearly so easily won over. Nor did the Seligmans exert much influence over the Jewish community as a whole. As a result, even the staid *New York Times*, which generally supported Grant and opposed ethnic appeals, warned in June of a possible "wholesale defection" on the part of Jews. That, it feared, "would endanger the election of Grant and Colfax in Illinois, and render the election of the Democratic ticket in Indiana certain beyond a doubt."[27]

"What can be done?" Joseph Medill, the Republican editor of the *Chicago Tribune*, asked Grant's longtime friend and supporter Congressman Elihu B. Washburne of Illinois, likely in response to articles in the *Times* and elsewhere. "The Jews of Cincinnati and St. Louis are numerous enough to defeat our ticket in both cities, and they are strong enough to hurt us in Chicago also, as they include many of our most active Republicans." Unless Grant put the issue to rest with a strong public statement, he warned, "we shall lose large numbers of Jew [*sic*] votes . . . besides converting them into very active bitter opponents."[28]

Grant later admitted to having received "hundreds of letters" from Jews inquiring about his order. Refusing to budge from his principles ("I thought it would be better to adhere to the rule of silence as to all letters"), he answered none of them. As a result, just as Medill had feared, the Democrats bustled about "making a handle" of Grant's expulsion order "in all parts of the country."[29]

Spurring them on from his place behind the scenes may have been the longtime chair of the National Democratic Committee, financier August Belmont. Born and educated as a Jew in Germany, Belmont made a substantial fortune as a banker in New York, aided by his close ties to the Rothschilds. He married (in a church) the daughter of Commodore Matthew Perry. Though he raised his children as Episcopalians and maintained no formal connections to the Jewish community, his enemies still frequently reminded him that he was a "foreign born Jew." He therefore understood as well as any politician of his day that the "Jewish issue" could be a potent weapon in the Democrats' campaign arsenal.[30]

The Democratic Speaker's Hand-book, prepared by the party for its loyal supporters, trumpeted that weapon. It devoted three double-column small-print pages to "General Grant on our Hebrew Fellow Citizens," recounting the episode to the bulk of Democrats who knew nothing about it. The section concluded with lines that the handbook likely expected party speakers on every stump to echo: "Violating trade, indeed! Why, that order was violated everywhere. . . . No; the Jews were persecuted because they were Jews, and nothing else." The handbook also reprinted an anti-Grant statement signed by two hundred Jews in St. Louis opposing the election of "such a man." Obliquely admitting that most American Jews were unaffected by the order, the St. Louis Jews nevertheless predicted that there would be "as few Israelitic (!) votes cast for General Grant next November as he had occasion to make arrests under his famous order." The handbook even reprinted the court proceedings in Jesse Grant's long-forgotten court case against the Mack brothers. It wondered darkly (and baselessly) whether it was "in view of this arrangement" between the Mack brothers and Grant's father, "and in order that it might be as profitable as possible, that General Grant issued his inhuman order of December 17, 1862, requiring all Jews to be expelled from his department?"[31]

Democratic newspapers soon embellished the story of Grant and the Jews with far-fetched tales that purported to "explain" the general's hostility toward Jews "as a class" based upon earlier incidents from his life, when individual Jews supposedly took advantage of his business naïveté. According to one widely repeated account, a Jew named Rosenthal, who was in the pork trade in Bellevue, Iowa, discovered that Grant, then trying his hand at that business, "knew no difference between the price of light and heavy hogs." Using a clever ruse, Rosenthal sold Grant all of his light hogs for the dearer price of heavy ones, and "it was not half an hour before every body nearly was splitting with laughter" at the Jew's craftiness. The transaction, according to the storyteller, greatly embittered Grant against "the old tribes of Israel," and "this is undoubtedly the whole cause of the expulsion of Jews from his camp." The tale echoed popular anecdotes concerning Grant's string of embarrassing business failures prior to the Civil War, toyed with well-known taboos concerning Jews and pork, and portrayed Jewish merchants as clever but utterly unscrupulous. For all that it reveals about cultural stereotypes, however, the story was soon shown to be the work of a "notorious rebel sympathizer," and the Rosenthal in question, who had been living in Bellevue at the time, indignantly insisted that it was "a lie from beginning to end."[32]

Another fabulous tale, published under the headline "Why Grant Issued His Order Against the Jews," was no less false, though even more revealing:

A prominent Jew cotton dealer of Cincinnati made a bargain with Grant for the getting out of five hundred bales of cotton from the Black River country assisted by the Second Wisconsin Cavalry. The Jew offered, as was the custom, one-fourth of the profits. Grant wanted more, and at last the Jew offered an eighth, which Grant accepted. The cotton was got out and shipped to Memphis and sold. The Jew, faithful to his promise, met Grant with the proceeds of the sale, and gave the General one-eighth of the profits and departed. Grant's Adjutant General, surprised at the smallness of the profits, spoke to the General about it, who was so exasperated on learning that one-eighth was less than one-fourth, that he within that hour issued the order expelling all Jews from the lines, and to this day has never forgiven the entire race for his own stupidity.[33]

While on the surface this tale, too, showed a shrewd, somewhat unscrupulous Jew taking advantage of an ignorant and naïve Grant, the story in this case employed authentic details from the historical episode involving Grant's father and the Mack brothers. The fact that the story confused Ulysses S. Grant with Jesse, and invented the "stupidity" that it attributed to the younger Grant, is less significant than that contemporary folklore in 1868 already linked the order expelling the Jews to the interactions between Grant and a "Jew cotton dealer of Cincinnati."

The Democratic newspapers that gave space to these and other stories concerning Grant and the Jews sought to cast doubt on Grant's fitness to be president. To the same end, a Wisconsin newspaper ridiculed Grant in verse:

> Who drove the Hebrews from his Camp,
> Into the Alligator swamp
> Where everything was dark and damp?
> Ulysses
> Who wrothy at those faithless Jews

Who kept "pa's" share of Cotton dues,
All further permits did refuse?
                                    Ulysses[34]

Other Democratic newspapers, like the provocatively named *Corinth Caucasian*, argued that only a loyal Democrat would frustrate the forces of Radical Reconstruction and preserve the prerogatives of the white race. They hoped that readers, Jewish and non-Jewish alike, would be dissuaded from voting for a candidate who could expel "Jews as a class," and vote, if only by default, for his opponent. That opponent was finally chosen early in July 1868. His name was Horatio Seymour, and he was a well-known New York politician.[35]

Nominated unanimously and very much against his will after twenty-one exhausting ballots failed to find an acceptable alternative, Seymour became the Democrats' compromise candidate to oppose Grant. The handsome former New York governor had publicly supported the Union war effort but opposed many of Abraham Lincoln's policies, including the emancipation of the slaves. In 1862, the platform he had run upon, when he won the state's governorship, denounced the Emancipation Proclamation as "a proposal for the butchery of women and children, for scenes of lust and rapine, and of arson and murder." Now Democrats called upon him "to drive from power the Radical cabal at Washington" and to declare the Reconstruction Acts "usurpations and unconstitutional, revolutionary and void."[36]

Seymour was a respected and well-liked conservative aristocrat known to favor limited government. His running mate, Francis P. Blair of Missouri, was more hotheaded. Although he had fought valiantly for the Union in the Civil War, he later fought equally determinedly against Reconstruction and any form of equality for the freed slaves. He promised, if elected, "to prevent the people of our race . . . from being driven out of the country or trodden under foot by an inferior and semi-barbarous race."[37]

The original caption to this 1868 Thomas Nast cartoon read:
*"We regard the Reconstruction Acts (so called) of Congress
as usurpations, and unconstitutional, revolutionary,
and void."—Democratic Platform*

With all the candidates finally in place, the 1868 election became something of a national referendum on Reconstruction and Black suffrage.
Thomas Nast, in a cartoon entitled "This Is a White Man's Government," captured the centrality of these themes by depicting the stalwarts
of the Democratic coalition—Democratic chair August Belmont, Confederate general Nathan Bedford Forrest, and an anonymous Irish immigrant workingman—all stomping on a Black veteran of the Union army
reaching out for the ballot box.[38] Complex economic issues at stake in the
election, such as the value of debased greenbacks and whether govern-

ment bonds would be repaid in gold, divided members of both parties and were in any case too abstruse for most voters to understand. By contrast, emotional issues concerning formerly rebellious states and recently freed slaves engaged every voter's attention. These issues upped the ante for Jews who choked at the thought of voting for Ulysses S. Grant but strongly supported Republican policies on Reconstruction. Should they vote for a party they considered bad for the country just to avoid voting for a man who had been bad to the Jews? The closer the election drew, the more heated rhetoric within the Jewish community became.

Simon Wolf, in a widely reprinted letter, insisted that Jews should always vote their principles. However ill-worded Grant's order might have been, that was no reason, he exclaimed, "why American citizens should be betrayed from their allegiance to principles, and turn to a party that advocated the reverse of what is right and true."[39] Henry Greene-baum, a banker and liberal Jewish leader from Chicago who had raised a Union regiment during the Civil War and was a proud proponent of social justice, completely agreed. He criticized Grant for prejudice ("if the nomination of a presidential candidate had been left to [R]epublican Jews there would have been a different choice") but nevertheless insisted that his faith led him "to regard *all* men as brothers," an indication that his definition of inclusiveness stretched far beyond that of the Democrats. To vote against the Republican Party, he warned, meant "impeding the progress of history."[40]

By contrast, Moses Ezekiel of Richmond, a Confederate veteran and budding sculptor (he would later produce a parade of Confederate war monuments) insisted that Jewish religious principles, as he understood them, required him to vote against Grant. "The Jew who does not with all his heart, soul and means, oppose the election of this second Pharaoh," he wrote, echoing one of Judaism's watchwords, "deserves to be publicly branded as a renegade to his faith." A writer in New York's *Hebrew Leader* summoned another biblical metaphor in encouraging Jews to oppose

Grant. Recalling the story of the ancient Amalekites, cursed by God for attacking Israel when it was vulnerable, he invoked the first words of the biblical injunction against Amalek from the book of Deuteronomy (25:17): "Remember what Amalek did unto you."[41]

Similar insistence upon religious duty—directed *negatively* against Grant, rather than *positively* in support of Horatio Seymour and the principles of his party—underlay unprecedented public gatherings by Jews in Memphis, Nashville, Atlanta, St. Louis, and Los Angeles. The gathering in Memphis, described as "large and enthusiastic," resolved that Grant was "a man unfit for the high position to which he aspires, and incapable of administering the laws to all classes with impartiality and without prejudice." Attendees pledged themselves as "Israelites who have respect for our honor and religion, pride for our race and love for our country to use every honorable means in our power to defeat the election of . . . U. S. Grant." One enthusiastic speaker, doubtless seeking to avenge Grant's occupation of Memphis during the Civil War, went further, thrilling the crowd with the suggestion that "if there was any high place to which the Jews would, perhaps, assist in elevating a man who had so foully abused them it would be to a place corresponding with that upon which Haman ended his career"—meaning, the gallows.[42] Atlanta's Jewish merchants boldly agreed. They erected a transparency on Whitehall Street that proclaimed: "The Jews will defeat Grant as they defeated Haman. The Jews will elevate Grant to office as they elevated Haman."[43]

Contemporary readers, recalling the prominent role Jews played in the civil rights movement of the twentieth century, may be surprised by the public support Jews gave to the anti-Black, openly racist Democratic Party in the wake of the Civil War. In the nineteenth century, however, Jews were divided regionally and politically; no one ideology defined them. Just as they resembled their neighbors in their attitudes toward slavery before the Civil War, so they resembled them in the war's immediate aftermath. What distinguished the 1868 election was that more

Jews than ever before *justified* their political loyalties on the basis of their religion. They campaigned as Jews.

America had never before witnessed such a public display of power on the part of Jews. Back in 1840, some American Jews had cautiously arranged public meetings in support of fellow Jews persecuted in Damascus. In 1858–59, they more enthusiastically joined a worldwide and ultimately unsuccessful campaign for the release of Edgardo Mortara, a six-year-old Italian Jewish boy who had been secretly baptized as an infant by his nursemaid in Bologna, and as a consequence was torn from his home and handed over to the Catholic Church. Domestically during the Civil War, Jews campaigned successfully, if largely behind the scenes, to broaden the military chaplaincy law, which initially restricted chaplains to those who were regularly ordained ministers "of some Christian denomination," so that non-Christians, Jews in particular, could also minister to troops. Most important of all, of course, American Jews succeeded during the Civil War in having General Orders No. 11 revoked. But these and other short-lived political engagements paled in comparison to the many attempts in 1868 to bring Jewish power to bear on an American presidential campaign. The question was whether group politics of this sort was appropriate.[44]

In the wake of their political emancipation in Europe, many Western and Central European Jews came to eschew the exercise of Jewish power through group politics of any sort. Sephardic leaders in London as late as 1819 went so far as to threaten excommunication to anyone who even voted in an election, much less took sides on a political question. Even after they received their rights as a group, often in the form of special legislation such as a "Jew Bill," Jews were expected to exercise those rights, if at all, solely as individuals. The last thing they wanted to do was to stir up old antisemitic canards about how they formed a state within a state, caring more about their fellow Jews than about their country. So as to protect their rights as individuals, they learned to piously insist that they no longer voted on the basis of any interests that they shared with fellow Jews.⁴⁵*

In America, where the Constitution treated them as equals and never mentioned the word "Jew" at all, immigrant Jews tended to follow these same carefully nurtured political habits. These were elaborated in four unwritten rules that came to define "proper" Jewish political behavior. The wisdom of these rules was likely reinforced in Jewish minds when they observed how viciously the Know-Nothing Party attacked Catholic political involvements in the 1850s, threatening to limit Catholic immigration and naturalization. Prudently, Jews forswore such involvements, binding themselves to the most straitlaced standards of group politics:

1. Jews may not band together in separate political clubs.
2. Rabbis or lay leaders have no right to advise the community on how to vote.
3. Jewish agencies must not use their influence to promote Jewish aspirants to political office.
4. Jews may not support a candidate just because he happens to be Jewish.⁴⁶

To avoid breaking these rules, the Jews of Memphis, in publicly opposing Grant, went out of their way to underscore that they were not motivated by "any political or party purpose."⁴⁷ But saying so did not make it so. Oftentimes, the Jews who forswore group politics the most loudly actually spent a great deal of time promoting Jewish political interests behind the scenes. To them and their descendants, well into the twentieth century, Jewish politics, the raw exercise of Jewish power, was akin to sexual

---

* Fascinatingly, a letter to the London *Jewish Chronicle* challenged these pieties based on American Jewry's example. In justifying a call for readers to vote against the apostate Joseph d'Aguilar Samuda, who was running for Parliament, "F.S.C.L." observed, "No one blames the American Jews for uniting to defeat the election of General Grant because he ventured to insult their brethren and their faith [July 24, 1868, p. 4]."

intercourse: practiced openly, it was embarrassing and shameful; done discreetly, behind closed doors, it was natural and legitimate.[48]

This explains why two of the most widely publicized critiques of American Jewish political activity in 1868 were written by two of the most politically active American Jews. Simon Wolf, who interceded with politicians regularly on behalf of Jewish interests, insisted that Jewish group interests simply did not exist. "We are not Jews in any political sense," he declared. "Accursed will be the day when Jews as a class commit the unpardonable crime of becoming sectarian in their politics." Taking his position to its logical extreme, he proclaimed, utterly unpersuasively, that Jews "are not Jews except to God; we are to the country what Mr. Smith, Mr. Jones or Mr. Brown are—citizens."[49]

Samuel Myer Isaacs, who played a central role in Jewish political affairs as a founder of the Board of Delegates of American Israelites, delivered the same message through his well-respected New York newspaper, the *Jewish Messenger*. "Judaism has nothing in common with partisan politics," he wrote in an article that the *New York Times*, among others, reprinted approvingly. He urged Jews "to give no countenance to any movement calculated to involve the Hebrews as a body in any political contest" and opposed both Jewish public meetings against Grant and the establishment of pro-Grant Jewish political clubs. Revealingly, he described this as the position of "sensible Jews" and "the better class of Israelites." He associated overt displays of Jewish political power, at least by implication, with the tawdry activities of lower-class voters.[50]

The more vexing question in 1868—and no less relevant today—was the question of multiple loyalties. Those who injected General Orders No. 11 into the presidential campaign plainly sought to appeal to Jewish voters on the basis of their special interests. But was it legitimate for Jews to base their vote on such considerations? Or, in selecting a presidential candidate, should they—and Americans generally—cast aside all special interests and consider only the national interest? More to the point, should General Orders No. 11 singlehandedly determine how Jews vote, or

Rabbi Liebman Adler

ought they, as responsible citizens and voters, to weigh up the totality of issues facing the country before making up their minds?

Two of America's most distinguished Reform rabbis debated this very question through the newspapers. Liebman Adler, the rabbi of Chicago's oldest synagogue, often known by its initials, K.A.M., argued against voting on the basis of Jewish interests and in favor of what he considered broad American interests. Proud as he was of being a Jew, he explained, "it is different when I take a ballot in order to exercise my rights as a citizen. Then I am not a Jew, but I feel and act as a citizen of the republic." On Election Day, he insisted, "I do not ask what pleases the Israelites. I consult the welfare of the country." So much did his responsibilities as a citizen outweigh those of being a Jew that he provocatively declared he would vote even for the party of Haman (which is just what the Republican Party was in the eyes of many Jewish Democrats) if he believed that it would do the most for the welfare of the country and the advancement of human rights:

> If that party in whose hands I believe the welfare of the country, so far as the advancement of human rights was concerned, was the safest, were to place a Haman at the helm of state, and if the opposite party, whose nonexistence I believe would be better for humanity

and my country, were to place Messiah at their head, make Moses the Chief Justice, and call the Patriarchs to the Cabinet, I should say, "Prosper under Haman, my fatherland, and here you have my vote, even if all the Jew in me mourns."

For Rabbi Adler, the principles of the Republican Party, particularly the promise that "all men of all races should be equal," trumped other considerations. Must Jews like himself set aside their principles and change their vote, he asked, "since Grant has insulted us?" Answering his own question, he declared forthrightly that "if Grant is the best man for the Americans, he is the best man for us Israelites, despite General Order No. 11."[51]

Rabbi Isaac Mayer Wise could not have disagreed more. "If wrong is wrong, he who defends it is wicked," Wise acidly wrote in condemning those who advocated Grant's election. "Men of principle and character . . . have the solemn duty to speak, to resent indecencies, to plead their cause, and to stand up firmly and decidedly for their rights and their principles." In reply to those, like Adler, who raised the specter of multiple loyalties, he insisted that identities, in real life, could not so easily be compartmentalized:

> We have been trying quite seriously to make of our humble self two Isaac M. Wises—the one who is a citizen of the State of Ohio, and the other who is a Jew; but we failed and we failed decidedly; we could not destroy our identity nor could we double it. In consequence of this exertion and this failure, we have come to the conclusion, that it is a piece of sophistry to suggest that one should be the one-half of himself.

Wise concluded that responsible voters needed to weigh up their responsibilities as Jews and as citizens at one and the same time: "We bring both the Jew and the citizen to the public forum and to the synagogue, before our God and our country." Defending his focus on General Orders No. 11, he insisted that "civil and religious liberty is a sacred boon which must be protected against each and every aggression . . . we must speak and act according to the very dictates of conscience and conviction."[52]

No final decision ever resolved this debate. It rises anew, like the phoenix, every time some Jewish issue (most recently support for Israel) intrudes into a presidential campaign. The same intensity, many of the same arguments, and only differences in detail distinguish the debates in Grant's day from those in our own. Then as now, the tensions inherent in the term "American Jew"—embracing responsibilities to country and to fellow Jews—heighten the challenge of casting a presidential ballot. Nor are Jews alone in facing this dilemma. Parallel tensions face members of almost every ethnic, religious, and special interest group. Weighing up competing claims, establishing priorities among one's principles and concerns, and reaching a decision about whom to support can make voting an excruciatingly difficult if deeply self-revealing process.

In 1868, many pundits expected that after weighing and balancing all of these different factors the majority of American Jews would vote against Ulysses S. Grant and in favor of Horatio Seymour. Self-interest, a cardinal principle of America's individualistic ethos, seemed to demand no less. A journalist from the South who visited a national B'nai B'rith convention in late July 1868 reported that 90 percent of those in attendance "are heart and soul opposed to Grant." The correspondent of the London *Jewish Chronicle*, that same month, informed his readers that American Jews were "uniting to defeat the election of General Grant because he ventured to insult their brethren and their faith." By October, when many neutral observers were predicting that Grant would win the election, based on state and local election victories by Republicans in eight states, the Cleveland *Plain Dealer*, noticing the significance of Jewish votes in several key states, still offered the Democrats a ray of hope: "The Israelites in the States of Pennsylvania, Ohio, New York, and Indiana," it declared, "have it entirely in their own power to secure the election of Seymour and Blair and the defeat of Grant and Colfax." The *St. Louis Times* and Washington *National Intelligencer* agreed. Exaggerating the number of "Hebrew voters" by a factor of almost ten ("there are four or five hundred thousand Hebrew voters in the United States"), the newspapers predicted that "the Hebrew vote of the United States will certainly effect the overthrow of the dominant [Republican] party."⁵³

Precisely such predictions, even if wildly exaggerated, had already moved Ulysses S. Grant to act. In response to a letter from an influential B'nai B'rith leader and lawyer, Adolph Moses of Illinois, a Confederate veteran, Grant on September 14 dispatched a private letter to their mutual friend, former congressman Isaac Newton Morris, in which he unequivocally distanced himself from General Orders No. 11 and forswore prejudice. The confidential letter was not published at the time. Grant, according to Simon Wolf, did not want the public to believe that "he was catering for the good wishes and possible votes of American citizens of the Jewish faith"—that, apparently, was acceptable for him to do in private but not in public. Still, leading Jews undoubtedly saw the letter. After reading it, Moses, probably at the urging of Grant's staff, composed a long letter of his own that appeared on the front page of the *New York Times* (October 13, 1868) and in other newspapers, just as the election entered its home stretch. "I have . . . corresponded with Gen. Grant," Moses announced dramatically, and Grant had made "a reparation." Though Moses had earlier criticized Grant in print, he reported that having reviewed the question anew, he would now follow his "political inclinations" without reference to the "side issue" of Grant's order. "The best interests of our country," he proclaimed, "are subserved by the election of Gen. Grant, and I have no diffidence to declare it to the community."⁵⁴

Just ten days later, a published letter in the *New York Herald* (October 23, 1868) from another wavering Jewish Republican, David Eckstein, a bookkeeper in Cincinnati, revealed that he actually had spoken to Grant for nearly two hours and was likewise now satisfied with the general's response. Indeed, Grant's explanations concerning General Orders No. 11 were, in Eckstein's optimistic view, "sufficient to remove and obliterate every vestige of objection against him on the part of every fair-minded and reasonable Israelite." He urged Jews to offer "hearty support" both to Grant and to "the party which put the General in nomination."[55]

What impact these and other last-minute endorsements made on Jewish voters is impossible to know. What really mattered were the results of the November 3 election, and when they were tallied, Grant emerged the winner by a healthy margin of 309,584 votes and 134 electoral votes. Except perhaps in New York, where Grant lost by precisely 10,000 votes and fraud was suspected, the Jewish vote could not have made much difference anywhere. Ohio and Pennsylvania, two states where Jewish voters were supposed to help the Democrats, both went Republican by comfortable margins. The vote in Indiana was closer, but the Jewish vote in that state was too small to make a difference. The more than 500,000 African American votes cast, especially in the South, most of which naturally went to Grant, made much more of a difference in the totals and may actually have swung the election in Grant's favor.[56]

Contemporaries disagreed as to how Jews finally voted. The Cleveland *Daily Herald* argued that Jews "were not deceived" by the campaign against Grant, "and very little attention was paid by them to the clamor." The *New York Times*, by contrast, estimated that "nearly the entire body of voting Israelites" voted against Grant.[57] All that we know for certain is that a young Jewish student at Yale University named Louis Ehrich, later a prominent collector and dealer of art, agonized over the question of how to cast his first presidential ballot. In the end, he voted Democratic. "My nation is too dear to me," he explained in his diary, "to allow me to respect one who injured it."[58]

A fitting epilogue to the tumultuous battle for the Jewish vote appeared in newspapers across the country during the final week of November. With the election behind him, Ulysses S. Grant permitted his private letter to Isaac Newton Morris concerning General Orders No. 11 to be handed over to the press. It told Jews just what they wanted to hear from the president-elect: *"I do not pretend to sustain the Order."* While Grant's self-serving explanation—"The order was issued and sent without any reflection and without thinking of the Jews as a sect or race"—did not actually bear close scrutiny, Jews were thrilled with the general's forthright, unambiguous, and appropriately italicized concluding declaration: "*I have no prejudice against sect or race, but want each individual to be judged by his own merit.* Order No. 11 does not sustain this statement, I admit, but then *I do not sustain that order.* It never would have been issued if it had not been telegraphed the moment it was penned, and without reflection."[59]

After months of bitter internecine political battling, Jews cheerfully united in praise of Grant's "noble and generous" letter, and understandably so. By declaring that "I do not sustain that order," Grant confessed misdeed and allied with values that, in the Civil War's wake, liberal Americans cherished above all others: freedom for all, malice toward none. Prejudice toward Jews, the president-elect had come to understand, was as unacceptable as prejudice toward Blacks. In atoning, his letter articulated a higher vision for Americans: "I . . . want each individual to be judged by his own merit."

Isaac Mayer Wise, who was the first to receive and publish Grant's letter, felt sure that it "would be read with pleasure by all of our readers." B'nai B'rith leader Benjamin F. Peixotto, who admitted to voting against Grant, rejoiced to the *New York Times* at how the letter "exonerates Gen. Grant from the imputation of prejudice and intolerance against the Jews, so long believed to be one of his characteristics." *The Occident*, now edited by Mayer Sulzberger, a future Pennsylvania judge, perceptively viewed the letter as "a guide for those who so easily fall into [Grant's] errors, but are so far from imitating his virtues."[60]

What the *Times* characterized as this "frank and manly confession" lifted the taint of "Haman" from upon Grant's shoulders. It did much to rehabilitate his image in Jewish eyes, restored Jews' confidence in the country's ideals, and added to the spirit of buoyant optimism that characterized American Jewish life as a whole at this time. Across the United States in the late 1860s, Jews were building magnificent synagogues and temples and looking forward with eager anticipation to a glorious "new era" characterized by liberalism, universalism, and interreligious cooperation. In calling for individuals to be judged according to their own merit, Grant's letter provided reassurance that he shared many of these same lofty goals.[61]

The so-called upstanding Israelites, many of them American-bred, who labored to bring forth this new era of religious good feeling were far removed from the "Jews as a class" that Grant had expelled in 1862 for trading, smuggling, and speculating. Some of them, particularly Simon Wolf and the Seligman brothers, had contributed significantly to the Republican victory. They were, for the most part, self-made men who had been born poor, worked hard, and succeeded—just like the president-elect himself. The question, as Ulysses S. Grant now prepared for his inauguration, was how his future relationship with these upstanding Israelites would inform his relationship with Jews and America at large.

4

"To Prove Impartiality Towards Israelites"

Ulysses S. Grant was forty-six years old when he stepped forward, on March 4, 1869, to take his oath of office. He was, at that time, the youngest person ever inaugurated as president of the United States. Physically unimpressive but steely in his determination, adorned in an expensive black suit and somewhat reticent, as if conscious of the formidable challenges awaiting him, the general appeared the very embodiment of the nation's hopes. "Let us have peace," he had proclaimed when he accepted his party's nomination. What he had meant, one biographer explains, was "peace between North and South; peace between black and white; peace after years of war and political conflict."[1] Now, in a characteristically short and plainspoken inaugural address, he once more urged his countrymen to heal the nation's sectional wounds and guarantee Black Americans the right to vote. The great challenges posed by Reconstruction, he preached, needed to be approached "calmly, without prejudice, hate, or sectional pride." He called upon each citizen to "do his share toward cementing a happy union."[2]

The question of what a "happy union" entailed bedeviled Grant's presidency. During his years in the White House, Americans redefined "we the people" and debated anew who could be citizens and what citizenship meant. The bulk of this debate naturally focused upon the rights of people freed from slavery by the Civil War, but there was discussion, too, about Indians, Chinese, and even Gypsies (only a small number of whom lived in the United States at that time).[3]

The Inauguration Ball, Treasury Department, Washington D.C.,
"Upon the Arrival of President Grant and his Wife, 1868."

When it came to Jews, some in Congress actually sought to downgrade their status in post–Civil War society via a constitutional amendment intended to "more fully recognize the obligations of the Christian religion." Having concluded that the Civil War was punishment for "the absence of any adequate recognition of the sovereignty of God . . . in our Constitution," supporters sought to remake America into an explicitly Christian state. The National Reform Association, founded in 1864, had as its object to "declare the nation's allegiance to Jesus Christ and its acceptance of the moral laws of the Christian religion, and so indicate that this is a Christian nation." To this end, it proposed to rewrite the Preamble of the Constitution to read as follows:

> We, the people of the United States, humbly acknowledging Almighty God as the source of all authority and power in civil government, the Lord Jesus Christ as the Ruler among the nations, his revealed will as the supreme law of the land, in order to constitute a Christian government, and in order to form a more perfect union,

establish justice, insure domestic tranquility, provide for the common defense, promote the general welfare, and secure the inalienable rights and the blessings of life, liberty, and the pursuit of happiness to ourselves, our posterity, and all the people, do ordain and establish this Constitution for the United States of America.[4]

Senator B. (Benjamin) Gratz Brown of Missouri, the non-Jewish grand-nephew and namesake of prominent Jewish merchant Benjamin Gratz, of Lexington, Kentucky, became a leading congressional supporter of this amendment. Perhaps fearing that his Gratz family associations would harm his future political aspirations, he declared that "unless we become in very truth a Christian nation, all other nationality will be ephemeral and delusive."[5] Steady propaganda and regular national conventions during Grant's years in the White House sought to advance the "religious" amendment. The goal, declared the 1872 convention of the National Association to Secure the Religious Amendment to the Constitution of the United States, was for Americans to "finally settle the question of the relation of their government to Christianity."[6]

B. Gratz Brown

Much to Jews' relief (and thanks, in part, to their effective behind-the-scenes lobbying), the proposed amendment repeatedly failed to make it out of congressional committee. Senator Charles Sumner of Massachusetts actually withdrew his support for the amendment owing to objections from his "Hebrew friends."[7] Nor did the amendment win the support of Grant, who articulated a more pluralistic vision of America and whose religious proclivities were, in any case, somewhat latitudinarian. Meanwhile, the Fourteenth Amendment to the Constitution broadened the definition of citizenship, to embrace "all persons born or naturalized in the United States." The Fifteenth Amendment went further, extending the franchise to millions, most of them male ex-slaves, who had never been permitted to vote before. Between them, these two amendments greatly broadened the constitutional definition of "we the people," just as Grant and his party had hoped. As for the position of Jews in American life, it remained, from a legal perspective, undiminished.

In other ways, the position of Jews during the Grant years dramatically improved. The new president reached out to Jews, appointing them to government positions they could never have aspired to hold before. In so doing, he sought to atone for General Orders No. 11 and to prove that, as the nation's chief executive, he was just what he had promised to be: without prejudice, eager for "each individual to be judged by his own merit." His policy of rapprochement with the Jewish community also cohered with his general policy of reconciliation, seeking to abate sectional and interracial tensions. As a result, Jewish participation in government expanded during Grant's presidency. Policies that the new president may initially have undertaken to reward Jewish supporters, improve his image with Jews, and win Jews back to the party of Lincoln ended up empowering the American Jewish community and opening the doors of government service to people who had previously been excluded from its ranks.

Jews held more government offices than ever before under Grant, and the government also displayed marked new sensitivity to Jewish interests. Instead of America becoming officially Christian, as supporters of the "religious amendment" had hoped, Judaism itself became a recognized American religion. This naturally posed a challenge to Americans who believed themselves to be "God's New Israel," rightful inheritors of the Jewish mantle. While Christian triumphalism of this type by no means disappeared during the Grant years, Judaism won increasing recognition and experienced a brief golden age.

The first tentative steps in this direction took place just two days after the inauguration when Grant's earliest and most tireless Jewish supporter, Simon Wolf, dispatched a three-sentence letter to the new president requesting a job. "I have the honor to apply for a position in the foreign service of the Government," Wolf began. Evincing pride in all three elements of his hybrid identity, he described himself as "a German by birth, an Israelite in faith, and . . . a thorough American by adoption." "Should I be appointed," he promised, "I will ever aim to uphold the dignity and integrity of the Government, and reflect credit upon the Country that has so kindly protected me." Supporting Wolf's application was a warm letter of recommendation (addressed to Missouri's Senator, Carl Schurz) from the German-Jewish leader Isidor Bush of St. Louis, a prominent Republican. He praised Wolf's character, boldness, amiability, and learning, recalled the young lawyer's warm and able support for Grant during the campaign, and vouched for his popularity, "especially among Israelites." "If Presid[en]t Grant wants to prove his impartiality towards Israelites and to disprove any unfriendliness attributed to him on account of Order No. 11," Bush shrewdly advised, "there is probably no better opportunity than by appointing Mr. Simon Wolf to the position for which I am informed, he is an applicant."[8]

Applications by the hundreds flooded Grant's desk in the early days of his administration. Like most successful politicians, the new president expected to fill vacant positions with acquaintances and supporters, so as to cement his hold on power and reward his friends. Patronage officially dominated most levels of government in the United States until the creation of the nonpartisan civil service in 1883. Before then, the principle articulated back in 1832 by New York's Senator William Learned Marcy held firm: "To the victor belongs the spoils."

Wolf did not have to wait long to receive his slice of these spoils. John A. Rawlins, Grant's longtime friend, onetime assistant adjutant general (back in 1862, he had countersigned General Orders No. 11), and now the secretary of war, advocated for him. So did Republican congressman Albert Gallatin Riddle of Ohio, who had known Wolf as a lawyer. In gratitude for Wolf's "ardent" services to the party during the election, especially his efforts "to overcome the reluctance of the Israelites," and perhaps also in recognition of his political and administrative skills, Grant nominated him, on April 17, not to the foreign service post that he had requested, but to a position more conveniently close to home, in Washington. He named him "Recorder of Deeds for the District of Columbia."9

Writing years later in his autobiography, Wolf modestly insisted that he did not "seek or covet" this office, and "determined . . . to decline the honor." He claimed that only when he learned that a protest had been lodged with the Senate Committee of the District of Columbia concerning the appointment of a Jew did he change his mind. If such a protest was made, however, no reference to it survives and its effect was nil. The Senate reported favorably upon the nomination a mere three days after it was announced. Wolf had initially hoped for a better appointment: being in the foreign service was both more exciting and more lucrative than being recorder of deeds. But he was apparently persuaded to accept the morsel that was offered him, and likely used the excuse of an antisemitic protest to save face. Regardless, his appointment was formally ratified by the Senate on April 30, 1869, and he took office on May 15.[10]

The office of recorder of deeds, created by Congress in 1863, was charged with recording and preserving "all deeds, contracts, and other instruments in writing affecting the title or ownership of any real estate or personal property" in the District of Columbia. The job was mind-numbing but hardly arduous, and the most routine labor was handled by lowly clerks. In addition to overseeing them, and ensuring that the office ran smoothly and efficiently, Wolf found that he had a more important role to play in the administration, as he recalled Grant himself explaining to him when they met. "I learn that you represent your co-religionists [and] that you also stand well with the German-American element," Grant told him. "I may want to see and consult you often." Wolf subsequently calculated that "no one . . . except those immediately surrounding him or the members of his Cabinet, saw President Grant oftener" than he did. Discounting Wolf's propensity to self-aggrandize and exaggerate, the record nevertheless discloses that he found numerous opportunities to intervene with Grant on behalf of individual Jewish office seekers as well as causes important to the Jewish community. To a president eager for "reconciliation," Wolf became primary adviser on Jewish (and occasionally on German-American) affairs. No previous American president ever appointed a Jew to so high a position of trust, and none before Grant ever sought to have a Jew in his administration to represent his "co-religionists" before the government.[11]

Years later, Wolf proudly reminded the *New York Times* that, as recorder, he "was the first public officer to give a colored man a clerkship." This was in line with Grant's official policy during Reconstruction, and the "colored man" in question was one of the sons of the ex-slave and prominent abolitionist leader Frederick Douglass, a Republican stalwart. By then, Civil War–era fears that freedom for Blacks would lead to persecution of Jews had been completely forgotten. "A Jew," Wolf piously proclaimed, "must not have any prejudice." In 1881, three years after Wolf had departed, President James Garfield appointed Frederick Douglass himself to be recorder of deeds. "I held the office of Recorder of Deeds of the District of Columbia for nearly five years," Douglass recalled in his autobiography. "Having, so to speak, broken the ice by giving to the country the example of a colored man at the head of that office, it has become the one special office to which, since that time, colored men have aspired." Thus, as happened so often in American history, a blow against discrimination that benefited Jews was subsequently extended to benefit Blacks. Prominent African Americans continued to occupy the office of recorder of deeds continuously until it was transformed into a civil service position in 1952.[12]

Reputedly, Ulysses S. Grant sought to appoint Jews to positions far more significant than that of the recorder of deeds during the first term of his administration. Banker and longtime family friend Joseph Seligman, according to the testimony of his son, Isaac, was invited by Grant to become secretary of the Treasury, an appointment that would have made him the first Jewish cabinet member in U.S. history. Grant's initial choice for the Treasury post, prominent retailer Alexander Stewart, ran afoul of an old statute barring from the position any person "concerned or interested in carrying on the business of trade or commerce." Seligman, had his nomination gone forward, might have fallen prey to the same ill-considered statute. But according to his son, "the bank needed him, and his brothers begged him to let politics and public office alone." Grant therefore appointed Massachusetts congressman George S. Boutwell to the job. Thirty-seven more years would pass before Oscar S. Straus, in 1906, became the first Jew to serve in an American presidential cabinet as secretary of commerce and labor under Theodore Roosevelt.[13]

Nothing daunted, Grant reportedly attempted to appoint another Jew, Washington, D.C., publisher and bookstore owner Adolphus S. Solomons, as "governor" of the District of Columbia, during the brief period when the nation's capital was administered like a territory. Solomons, in 1863, had privately criticized General Orders No. 11 as "ill-liberal and un-lawful," but later became friendly with Grant, and in 1871 was elected to the District's House of Delegates, chairing its committee on ways and means. According to an unpublished report, probably written by his son-in-law, N. Taylor Phillips, Solomons was offered the district's governorship by Grant and declined it. As a religiously observant Jew, he

Adolphus Solomons

explained, he felt "that his observance of the seventh day Sabbath would be incompatible with the duties of his office."[14]

Even if these family traditions cannot be confirmed by official records, their existence is deeply revealing. In a country where ex-slaves, during Reconstruction, held high elective and appointive offices, the idea that Jews might similarly be considered for such positions no longer seemed radical. In fact, Grant did, at Wolf's behest, appoint a whole series of Jews to other governmental positions. For example, David Eckstein of Cincinnati, who, as we have seen, had valiantly supported Grant in 1868, became consul at Victoria, British Columbia. Nathan Newitter became consul at Osaka, Japan. Charles Mayer became district attorney for the Middle District of Alabama. Jacob Sterne, a Confederate veteran, became deputy postmaster in Jefferson, Texas. Years later, Wolf calculated that "more than fifty appointments were made by President Grant at his request." The Jews among those fifty were friends and acquaintances, people who supported the president and his party, and could be counted upon to be dependable and loyal—critical attributes of patronage appointees to this day. Like the "upstanding Israelites" who had campaigned for Grant in 1868, the Jews who received appointments from him were refined professionals, the kind of self-made men whom the president prized above all others. In a conscious effort to demonstrate his own lack of prejudice and to supply "the best answer" to Jews who considered him an enemy, Grant, according to Wolf, appointed "more Israelites to office than any other President since the founding of the Government."[15]*

Two of Grant's Jewish appointments stood out, attracting special notice. The first was Wolf's longtime friend Edward S. Salomon, whom Grant appointed governor of the Washington Territory. He became the first self-identifying American Jew to sit in a governor's chair (David Emanuel, governor of Georgia in 1801, never identified himself as a Jew). A native of Schleswig, Salomon seemed to embody the American Dream. He immigrated to Chicago as a seventeen-year-old, studied law, and won election as an alderman at the remarkably young age of twenty-four. During the Civil War, he distinguished himself in battle several times, including at Gettysburg, and won an honorary ("breveted") promotion for "distinguished gallantry and meritorious services" to the rank of brigadier general (one of only a handful of Jews in the Union army to achieve that rank). He then served as clerk of Cook County. At the time of his appointment, on January 10, 1870, Salomon, then thirty-two, knew absolutely nothing about the Washington Territory—not even its whereabouts—but the position paid a respectable $3,000 a year (more

---

* Probably the youngest Jew who owed his career to a Grant appointment was sixteen-year-old Albert A. Michelson. Upon the recommendation of Nevada congressman Thomas Fitch and Vice Admiral David D. Porter, Grant, on June 28, 1869, appointed him to the U.S. Naval Academy at Annapolis. Only ten appointments-at-large were allotted to the president, and Michelson was his eleventh appointment. But the strong recommendations that Michelson received, coupled with Congressman Fitch's observation that "these people [the Jews] are a powerful element in our politics, the boy who is uncommonly bright and studious is a pet among them, and I do most steadfastly believe that his appointment at *your* hands, would do more to fasten these people to the Republican cause, than anything else that could be done," brushed such obstacles aside. Michelson, in 1907, won America's first Nobel Prize in Physics. Dorothy Michelson Livingston, *The Master of Light: A Biography of Albert A. Michelson* (New York: Charles Scribner's Sons, 1973), 22–27.

Edward Salomon,
governor of the Washington Territory, 1870

than $50,000 in today's money), as well as expenses, and was a shrewd "two-for-one" patronage appointment; it pleased both Germans and Jews. Even Grant's longtime opponents cheered it. "The appointment," Rabbi Isaac Mayer Wise gushed, "shows that *President* Grant has revoked *General* Grant's notorious order No. 11." Like so many subsequent (and more prominent) appointments through the years that propelled Jews through glass ceilings—the first Jewish Supreme Court justice (1916), the first Jewish secretary of state (1973), the first Jewish candidate for the vice presidency on a major party ticket (2000), and so forth—the honor redounded to the benefit of all Jews. They basked in Salomon's reflected glory and hoped that his achievement would make it easier for them to fulfill their highest aspirations as well.[16]

As governor, Salomon promoted immigration, education, and equal representation in government. He also preached in 1871 at the tiny Yom Kippur service held for the seven Jewish families of Olympia, Washington. While his words on that day, set aside for Jews to atone for their sins, have not been preserved, his thoughts may easily be guessed at. Just two months earlier he had been caught, red-handed, using public funds for private gain.[17]

On July 23, a Treasury agent named R. H. Leipold had conducted a surprise audit of the state's Treasury. He found some $30,500 missing (equivalent to about $600,000 today), much of it ($28,000) easily accounted for through promissory notes discovered in the governor's private safe documenting loans to his brother-in-law and assorted political friends for land speculations. Such practices were all too common in post–Civil War America, a period one scholar has labeled "the era of good stealings." Many leading figures in the Washington Territory "borrowed" public funds to make short-term private loans and investments. Salomon, however, compounded his crime by desperately attempting to bribe Treasury agent Leipold. When that failed, he obtained short-term loans from bankers in Portland and made full restitution, but was apparently less than contrite. He explained to the bankers, according to one source, that with the money restored, "the agent would go away," previous practices could resume, and all would be well.[18]

The agent did not go away. Instead, he dispatched a detailed account of Salomon's misdeeds to the secretary of the Treasury. Meanwhile, an outraged Union veteran who somehow learned of these events sent a protest directly to Grant. Seeing the handwriting on the wall, Salomon, in January 1872, sent in his resignation to take effect three months later. Secretary of State Hamilton Fish was outraged: "Do you intend to allow him to remain in office until that time?" he inquired of Grant. "He ought to be removed at once." But Grant, ever loyal to those who served under him and mindful, perhaps, that he himself had not been removed after he expelled Jews from his war zone, permitted the young Jewish governor to save face.[19]

Years later, Simon Wolf, who certainly knew better, described Salomon (quoting a local Republican newspaper) as being "honest, fearless and capable." Jewish history books since then have generally echoed this assessment, recalling the first American Jewish territorial governor as an American Jewish "pioneer" and "patriot." Not one of the three major Jewish encyclopedias explains why he resigned his office when he did. By contrast, students of the Grant administration have remembered the

Salomon episode as a signal of the president's "curious attitude toward corruption in office." By not coming down hard on appointees who mis-used their positions for private gain, they contend, Grant conveyed the all-too-beguiling message that crime paid. Salomon's religion arguably worked to his advantage here. Grant may have feared the implications of a public scandal involving a highly placed Jew. He was working hard to win the Jewish community over, and knew from experience how quickly the jackals of prejudice could be set to howling. By allowing Salomon to resign quietly, he made it easier to nominate other Jews to positions of public trust.[20]

The same year that he nominated Salomon, Grant put forth the name of a second Jew for a responsible position that no Jew had ever held before. He appointed Dr. Herman Bendell, age twenty-seven, to be superinten-dent of Indian affairs for the Arizona Territory. Born in Albany, Bendell received his doctorate of medicine at the age of nineteen and served as a surgeon in the Civil War, rising to become head of the depot field hos-pital of the Army of the Potomac. Returning to Albany after the war, he established a medical practice and, like Wolf and Salomon, played an active role in the Jewish fraternal organization B'nai B'rith. While he had absolutely no experience with "Indian affairs," that was not what made his appointment noteworthy; the same was true of other aspirants to the office. The distinctive feature, particularly fascinating in terms of Grant's Christian-based Indian policy, was the fact that Bendell was a Jew.[21]

In his inaugural address, Grant had signaled that he favored a sympa-thetic new policy toward "the original occupants of this land—the Indi-ans." "I will favor any course toward them," he declared, "which tends to their civilization and ultimate citizenship."[22] At a time when many in the West, including his good friend William Tecumseh Sherman, promoted policies that tended toward the extermination of the "original occupants," Grant, with his broader Reconstruction-era vision of what it meant to be an American, appointed as commissioner of Indian affairs a full-blooded Seneca Indian, Ely S. Parker—formerly his military secretary and a

Ely S. Parker

well-educated Christian.* Grant ordered that Indians be treated as much as possible not on a tribal basis but as *individuals* responsible for their own actions. Ironically, this echoed Lincoln's response to General Orders No. 11. To condemn a class on account of a few sinners, Grant now understood, meant wronging the good with the bad.[23]

Parker, who sometimes styled himself "the Wolf" based on his Indian clan name, soon became for Native Americans what Simon Wolf was for Jewish Americans. Both men represented their communities in government, both mediated between their communities and the larger American public, and both served as role models, living proof that even the most "savage" or despised of minority groups could be upraised and transformed.[24]

---

* When Robert E. Lee surrendered at Appomattox Court House in 1865, Grant had introduced him to Parker. Noticing his dark features, Lee at first mistook him for a Black man and reportedly "flushed with indignation." Recognizing his mistake, he extended his hand and said, "I am glad to see one real American here." Parker, according to the account, took Lee's hand and replied, "We are all Americans." William H. Armstrong, *Warrior in Two Camps: Ely S. Parker, Union General and Seneca Chief* (Syracuse, N.Y.: Syracuse University Press, 1978), 108–10.

Together, Grant and Parker developed a policy aimed at Americanizing and Christianizing Native Americans. Where patronage and graft had characterized earlier pacification efforts, the new plan called for missionary agents from different Protestant denominations to be assigned to each tribe to oversee their needs and bring to them the blessings of Western civilization. Grant considered it "highly desirable" that "the aborigines . . . become self-sustaining, self-relying, Christianized, and civilized." He looked to missionary agents and to the new Board of Indian Commissioners to accomplish these goals. The wealthy, philanthropic, and all-Protestant members of the new board—at least one of whom, Felix Brunot, strongly supported the "religious" amendment to the Constitution—hardly needed much encouragement. "The religion of our blessed Saviour," they proclaimed, "is believed to be the most effective agent for the civilization of any people."[25]

Today, Jews and civil libertarians would hasten to challenge a policy like this as an obvious violation of Article VI of the Constitution ("no religious Test shall ever be required as a Qualification to any Office or public Trust under the United States") and, even more so, of the First Amendment's ban on the establishment of religion. In Grant's day, however, court cases based on religious liberty were few and far between. Seeking to forestall criticism, the government initially apportioned missionary appointments among eight different Protestant denominations, thereby ensuring that no single one was "established." Non-Protestants, however, remained firmly excluded from this "Christianization" campaign. Catholics protested, and over time their missionaries came to play an increasing role in Indian affairs, anti-Catholic prejudices notwithstanding. Jews, however, did not have any missionaries. Indeed, leading modern Jewish thinkers, like the German-Jewish philosopher Moses Mendelssohn, insisted that Judaism was distinct from Christianity in not being a missionizing religion at all. Since Jews likewise did not subscribe to "the religion of our blessed Saviour," they seemed destined to be shut out of the government's new Indian policy for, according to its calculus, religion trumped race. The goal of "Christianization" would thus deny even people who shared the *original* religion of the "blessed Saviour" but were not themselves Christians any role in supervising Indian affairs.[26]

Simon Wolf nevertheless recalled that he "saw no reason . . . why the Jewish faith should not also have a representative," and took personal credit for bringing the issue to Grant's attention. Other sources suggest that Grant acted in response to a more collective Jewish protest. Whatever the case, Grant once again proved sympathetic toward Jewish concerns for equality and ensured that Jews were included in his "Christianization" initiative after all. The appointment of Bendell simultaneously placated the Jewish community, since it placed one of their own in a position of authority over Native Americans, and freed the new appointee, whose job was to oversee "officers and persons employed by the government," from becoming directly involved with day-to-day missionizing efforts. "Let our Christian friends give themselves no uneasiness," the *Jewish Times* wrote approvingly soon after the appointment was announced. "The Jewish superintendent will not disturb the Christian missions much, nor will he attempt to make capital for the Jewish religion. . . . We suppose the President made the appointment to signify his sense of equity by recognizing the Jewish church, and according it the same privileges as to other denominations."[27]

The opposition of New York's Senator Roscoe Conkling (known in his day as "the great American quarreler") threatened to derail Bendell's nomination. Grant generally cleared appointments of New Yorkers with the powerful senator prior to making them, and Conkling was miffed that he had not been consulted about this one. The Catholic *Pilot* likewise sought to kill the nomination, warning that Bendell might "undo the work of the . . . missionaries" and calling upon "the Christian people, and the Catholics in particular" to protest against "an Israelite superintendent." But the Senate, on January 12, 1871, brushed aside these objections

Herman Bendell

and confirmed Bendell anyway. As soon as four Albany Jews put up the required $50,000 surety bond, the doctor took off for the West. He would later be remembered as the first Jewish settler of Phoenix, Arizona.[28]

Bendell, once ensconced in his new job, sent regular reports back to Washington on the conditions of Indians in the Arizona Territory. He deplored the lack of proper sanitation on the reservation of the Mohave Indians. He noted large numbers of syphilis cases, the product of fraternization between soldiers and Mohave women. He found medical care unsatisfactory and called for the establishment of "a proper hospital upon the reserve." He fought corruption among Indian suppliers, courageously going head-to-head with Arizona's leading Jewish merchants, the Goldwaters, in his insistence on following government regulations. He even, as a Jew, promoted "the introduction of missionaries among these wild children of the mountain." Christian missionaries, he advised the commissioner of Indian affairs, would "bring the most cruel savage on our continent . . . face to face with the highest element in our condition of civilization."[29]

The missionaries, however, did not return the compliment. John H. Stout, an agent to the Pima Indians selected and backed by the Dutch Reformed Church, confidentially warned Vincent Colyer, first secretary of the Board of Indian Commissioners, that Bendell was an "Israelite" who could not be trusted to advance the cause of Christianity. He encouraged his church to advocate the appointment of one of its own as superintendent of Indian affairs for the Arizona Territory, and to insist that the next superintendent "should be of our way of thinking." Eager to promote peace, General Oliver O. Howard, founder and president of Howard University and a leading advocate for the downtrodden, lauded Bendell following a fact-finding mission to Arizona, but nevertheless suggested that he be replaced by a "Dutch Reformed Churchman." A Washington, D.C., meeting of the Board of Indian Commissioners likewise praised Bendell for his work while condemning him for his faith. "Dr. Herman Bendell, Superintendent of Indian Affairs for Arizona, is a most excellent official, a man of splendid judgment, strict integrity, who has managed the affairs to entire satisfaction," Simon Wolf heard the commissioners conclude, "but unfortunately he is not a Christian." Whether this would have been enough to dismiss Bendell cannot be known, for in March 1873 he announced his resignation. He was getting married and sought to be closer to home. J. A. Tonner of the Dutch Reformed Church was immediately selected to succeed him. Thereafter, into the twentieth century, Jews were unofficially excluded from most aspects of Indian affairs. Policy makers denied religious "outsiders," like the Jews, any role in transforming Native Americans into "insiders."[30]

Grant, whose loyalty to those who served under him was legendary, compensated Bendell by appointing him consul to Helsingør (Elsinore), Denmark—a more suitable appointment for the newly married physician.[31] The president may have sought to signal, in this way, that those who carried out his policies toward the Indians would not be permitted to extend their prejudices into diplomatic appointments. Whatever the case, the appointment of Bendell, like the appointments of Salomon and Wolf and the attempted appointments of Seligman and Solomons, left no doubt as to Grant's overall attitude toward Jews. Far from excluding them, he now went out of his way to include them. During his administration, Jews won growing acceptance within American political life.

5

"This Age of Enlightenment"

For all of the domestic Jewish appointments that Grant made, his real test, Jews knew, would come in the international arena. How would the president respond if foreign governments persecuted and expelled the Jews? Less than nine months after his inauguration, such a test arrived in the form of a Russian replay of General Orders No. 11. Leading newspapers, including the *New York Times*, reported that two thousand Jews were being "removed from the Bessarabian frontier" to the Russian interior. They were charged, among other things, with smuggling.[1]

Prior to the Civil War, President James Buchanan had declared that the United States had "neither the right nor the duty . . . to express a moral censorship over the conduct of other independent governments." He therefore refused in 1858 to join the worldwide campaign on behalf of Edgardo Mortara, the young Italian Jewish boy who had been secretly baptized, torn from his home, and, in accordance with local law, handed over to the Catholic Church for upbringing. Realizing that American slave children were similarly being torn from their homes and handed over to new masters, and aware that under the tit-for-tat rules of international diplomacy other nations might choose to interfere in America's debate over slavery, Buchanan fell back upon a time-honored principle of international law: no country has the right to intervene in the internal affairs of another.[2]

The situation in Russia, in 1869, seemed to call for renewed application of this principle; it was an "internal affair." The expulsion of the Jews was justified on the basis of a tsarist edict, a ukase, dating back to 1825, that barred Jews from living within seven and one half miles (fifty versts) of any of Russia's borders. Since those borders had shifted on account of the 1856 Paris treaty that ended the Crimean War, tens of thousands of Jewish families now lived in the affected area, which included the city of Kishinev (now Chişinău), later the site of infamous anti-Jewish pogroms. However cruel the forced relocation of those Jews might be, it accorded with Russian law.[3]

America's Jews, incensed at Russia's discriminatory laws and moved by the plight of their persecuted coreligionists, nevertheless demanded action. They had not previously taken the lead in responding to persecutions of Jews abroad. Powerful Jews in Western Europe, most notably England's Sir Moses Montefiore, typically hastened to the defense of stricken Jews while American Jews cheered from afar. Now, having grown in numbers and gained in political experience, leaders of B'nai B'rith's Elijah Lodge in Washington, led by Grant's confidant Simon Wolf, resolved to act on their own. Working quickly, the lodge drew up an eloquently worded document that detailed the "cruel persecution" that Jews were experiencing in "primitive Russia," offered praise for Tsar Alexander II's otherwise "liberal and enlightened views," blamed "an ignorant and cruel peasantry" for the Jews' plight, and, most important, set forth a bold and innovative rationale explaining why, notwithstanding the traditional reluctance to interfere with the internal affairs of other nations, human rights considerations now mandated decisive government action:

[A]lthough we well know, that it is against the policy of this Government to interfere with the internal affairs of any other people, yet there are crimes committed in the name of municipal jurisdiction, that by their nature and magnitude become offences against humanity, and thus are violations and infractions of the law of nations. . . .

[I]t will be a hopeless task to endeavor to permanently unite the nations of the Earth in bonds of amity, unless one universal law of humanity is recognized. It is exacted in time of war of an enemy—is it foreign to the genius of our enlightened institutions to urge it on a friendly power in time of peace . . . ?

Is it too much to ask the United States to proclaim that henceforth it shall be an integral part of her intercourse with the nations, that international law recognizes *only*, as members of the family of nations those people who are guided by the unchangeable laws of a common humanity[?]

In a face-to-face meeting with President Grant, just three days after word of the persecutions reached the newspapers, Wolf and other leading Jews presented him with this forceful appeal and asked him "to represent to the Russian Government that this subject has been brought to the notice of the President of the United States" in the hope that he might use his influence to have the decision to expel the Jews "revoked or modified."[4]

Grant had every reason to decline this request. Russia, he knew, had stood by the United States during the Civil War and had sold Alaska to the United States on generous terms in 1867. It made little sense, from the perspective of American interests, to place that country's friendship with the United States at risk, especially at a time when tensions with England already ran high. The policy of non-entanglement in the internal affairs of other nations, moreover, had served America well. Even without the need to worry about foreign condemnations of American slavery, why change a policy that worked?

As if these two arguments were not persuasive enough, Grant surely knew that any comment on Russia's actions would inevitably renew discussion of his own actions, just seven years before, that uncomfortably resembled those of the Russians. Had not he, too, expelled "Jews as a class"? Indeed, the very language subsequently employed by the American diplomat and scholar Eugene Schuyler (translator of Turgenev and

Tolstoy) to justify Russia's actions to his superiors at the State Department closely resembled the language and the rationale of General Orders No. II. "The Jews who lived immediately on the frontier," the diplomat explained, "had little to lose and made large gains by smuggling goods into Russia, and by smuggling conscripts and refugees out of Russia. Until the last year there was an immense smuggling trade across this large frontier, which was entirely in the hands of Jews." "As a class," he reported, "they were thought to be lawbreakers and smugglers."⁵*

Notwithstanding these persuasive arguments for nonaction, Grant, increasingly sensitive to the rights of individuals and likely seeking to atone for the blot on his record that General Orders No. II represented, acted swiftly and decisively. "It is too late, in this age of enlightenment, to persecute any one on account of race, color or religion," he exclaimed. "He would take great pleasure," he said, "in being the medium to cause a revocation of the ukase, and would lay the appeal before the Cabinet about to assemble." He subsequently decided, according to the diary of Secretary of State Hamilton Fish, "that the subject be mentioned to the Russian minister with the expression of the hope that the Russian government may not find itself obliged to resort to such measures."⁶

Hamilton Fish did his best to thwart Grant's humanitarian impulse. He feared the implications of interference in Russia's internal affairs and was unmoved by B'nai B'rith's argument that human rights trumped long-standing diplomatic protocols. Indeed, Fish initially claimed—based on information he naively accepted from the Russian minister—that Jews in Russia "now enjoy all the civil and political privileges allowed to other subjects of whatever religious faith" and that the expulsion report

---

* Schuyler displayed little sympathy for Russia's Jews. In a private letter to his sister describing the Jews of Paltava, he complained that "they go about in the dirtiest and greasiest of garments, with brutish and disagreeable faces, their disgusting elfish curls hanging down over their temples." Richard J. Jensen, "The Politics of Discrimination: America, Russia and the Jewish Questions, 1869–1872," *American Jewish History* 75 (March 1986): 286.

rested "upon some misapprehension of fact, or upon some exaggeration of a less important incident." When updated information from Europe and behind-the-scenes interventions from Jewish leaders gave the lie to that excuse, Fish ordered the American ambassador to "make urgent but careful inquiry" into the matter. Beyond publishing the resulting inquiry, which was America's first official state paper concerning the situation and treatment of Jews in Russia, however, Fish did nothing. Neither he nor Grant intervened directly with the Russian authorities on Jews' behalf.[7]

That, in the end, hardly mattered. The B'nai B'rith petition and Grant's sympathetic response to it received wide publicity and were quoted by diplomats in their dispatches home. The Russian authorities postponed and then revoked their expulsion order, perhaps, as some claim, because it was too difficult to carry out logistically and would have damaged the local economy, but perhaps, too, because they feared an international outcry. Whatever the case, Americans understandably credited their own leaders, and especially Ulysses S. Grant, for achieving this happy result. Simon Wolf declared that the president's actions "answered the query of politicians as to whether he fosters prejudice against the Jews." The *New York World* found it "pleasing to see how different President Grant is from that General Grant who issued . . . an order suddenly exiling all the Jews from their homes within the territory occupied by his armies."[8]

The episode not only improved Grant's image, it also improved the image of Jews in the eyes of their neighbors. By joining with Grant in appealing to high-minded human rights claims, Jews looked to be shaping an America that explicitly promoted "one universal law of humanity." Long before such ideas gained currency in international circles, they were helping to bring about a key change in U.S. foreign policy, justifying interference in the internal affairs of other countries when human rights were at stake. In so doing, Jews distanced themselves from the immigrant peddlers and smugglers that Grant and so many others had once disdained. They fashioned themselves instead as champions of freedom, self-confident advocates of the rights of individuals, and defenders of persecuted Jews around the world.

Persecutions of Jews unfortunately continued, forcing American Jewish leaders to approach Grant again, this time on behalf of Jews in Romania. News of atrocities committed against Jews in that country reached the Jewish and non-Jewish press in the late 1860s, even before Grant's ascension to power. "Terrible Persecution of the Jews in Roumania," a *New York Times* headline screamed on June 14, 1867. The story, reprinted from the London *Times* and based on a telegram received from a Jewish eyewitness in the city of Jassy [now Iaşi], the former capital of Moldavia [Moldova], outraged Jews and non-Jews alike:

> In all the streets nothing is heard but the shrieks of the women and the weeping of the children of the banished Jews. We continue to be hunted down on all sides. The aged and the sick are bound in chains and dragged to some unknown destination. All our prayers for the protection of the law are rejected by the authorities. We are declared to be outlaws. The mobs are encouraged to exterminate us. It is only by means of prompt and efficacious succor that we can be saved from a frightful fate. Our eyes are turned to you our illustrious co-religionists. Save, save your wretched brethren of Moldavia![9]

Moldavia, which had united with Walachia in 1859 to form what became Romania, housed Jewish communities that dated far back in time. In the nineteenth century, these areas also attracted significant numbers of Jewish newcomers, especially during the era of Russian control, for immigration was easy and the opportunities for middle-class merchants seemed plentiful. Urbanization, when it occurred, brought with it the promise of further economic opportunity, but economic rivalries and religious hatred regularly conspired to deny Jews equality. In 1866, a new conservative regime took power that introduced or restored measures that legalized discrimination against the country's Jews, limiting where they could live, denying them the right to own land, and restricting the kinds of occupations that they could hold. Article 7 of the country's new constitution stated unambiguously that Romanian citizenship may be acquired by Christians only. Jews, even when native born, were deemed stateless foreigners (one minister called them a "social plague"). The regime forcibly deported hundreds of Jews and encouraged mob violence against thousands of others. One politician openly suggested that the best solution to the problem posed by Jews was to "drown them in the Danube."[10]

In early June 1870, American newspapers reported that "fearful massacres" of Jews were taking place all over Romania. The *San Francisco Bulletin* put the figure of those murdered at "a thousand men, women and children"; others estimated the toll to be much higher. The French Alliance israélite universelle, which kept close watch on Romanian Jewish affairs, dispatched hundreds of telegrams to Jewish communities around the world seeking support for the persecuted victims. "The fury of the population is terrible," it quoted one Jewish eyewitness as declaring. "We implore your aid." The *New York Times*, comparing the violence to the infamous St. Bartholomew's Day massacre of 1572 that had decimated France's Huguenot population, called upon the U.S. government to "do all in its power to check the hideous massacre." Meanwhile "leading Israelites" from around the country "arouse[d] their representatives in Congress to do all they can," and similar messages poured into the White House. Simon Wolf was reported to be "actively engaged all day in Executive and legislative circles" seeking intercession on behalf of Romanian Jews.[11]

Grant, in keeping with his new foreign policy priorities, moved swiftly. Paying a personal visit to the State Department, he instructed Hamilton Fish "to obtain full and reliable information in relation to this alleged massacre, and in the meantime to do all in his power to have the [neighboring] Turkish government stop such persecution." It was reliably reported that, with Grant's approval, the State Department would soon appoint "Adolphe Buchner, who is an Israelite," to serve as consul at Bucharest.[12]

Buchner, a resident of Bucharest and member of a significant Jewish family there, had previously served as secretary to the U.S. consul and maintained ties to the leaders of the Board of Delegates of American Israelites. Months earlier, when the consulship became vacant, he sought their aid in his quest to be made consul himself "in view of the moral influence that the nomination of a Hebrew as American Consul here might exercise upon the minds of our authorities." Now, with Jews and others clamoring for action, and Grant eager to prove himself a friend of human rights causes generally, especially those involving Jews, Wolf pushed Buchner's nomination onto the diplomatic fast track.[13]

Then, at the last moment, it was derailed. Owing to the astonishing intervention of a colorful rabbi named Haim Zvi Sneersohn, a descendant of the founder of the Hasidic movement today known as Chabad-Lubavitch, Grant made a far more daring appointment, subsequently described (with pardonable exaggeration) as "unique in diplomatic history." He appointed an American Jewish leader to be U.S. consul to Romania, and, recalling his approach to Indian affairs, included among the consul's duties "missionary work" for the benefit of Jews "laboring under severe oppression."[14]

Rabbi Haim Zvi Sneersohn,* in addition to being the great-grandson of Shneur Zalman of Liadi, the storied and much-revered founder of the Chabad-Lubavitch movement in Russia, was also the grandson of that family's most notorious black sheep, the founder's emotionally troubled son, Moshe, who to the movement's great embarrassment converted to Christianity in 1820. Perhaps to escape the stigma of what was then seen as the ultimate form of religious betrayal, Moshe's wife, son, daughter-in-law,

* The patronymic Sneersohn asserted descent from the family's rabbinic patriarch, Shneur Zalman. Family members over the years employed different English spellings for this name, including *Sneersohn*, the spelling used by Rabbi Haim Zvi Sneersohn; *Schneersohn*, the spelling used by the sixth Lubavitcher ("of Lubavitch") rebbe, Rabbi Joseph I. Schneersohn, when he arrived in the United States in 1940; and *Schneerson*, the spelling used by his son-in-law, the seventh and last rebbe, Rabbi Menahem Mendel Schneerson.

and grandchildren, including ten-year-old Haim Zvi, moved to the land of Israel in 1843–44 to begin life anew.[15]

From a young age, Haim Zvi displayed oratorical and linguistic skills, as well as a significant wanderlust, so from the age of eighteen he was made an emissary of Kollel Chabad and other Jewish philanthropic institutions in the land of Israel, raising money, among other things, for the shelters for the needy (*Batei Mahase*) that today house Yeshivat HaKotel in Jerusalem. Sneersohn's primary job was to collect funds and transmit them homeward, but as part of his fund-raising travels he played many other roles as well: teacher, preacher, pastor, missionary, diplomat, and more. He was especially keen to promote the return of Jews to the land of Israel in anticipation of the coming of the Messiah; like many Chabad followers, he expected redemption to occur imminently. But unlike today's Chabad emissaries, the so-called rebbe's army, he had no fixed base. His far-flung expeditions took him to different communities—including Syria, Egypt, Persia, Australia, England, and Romania—where he learned to inspire Jews and non-Jews alike.[16]

In 1869, apparently on his own initiative, the then thirty-five-year-old rabbi came to the United States. His goals were to raise funds through a nationwide lecture tour and to publicize his views on the coming redemption ("the finger of God points out to us that the day is not far distant when the grand deliverance will take place"). He also carried with him a political agenda: to lobby for the replacement of the American consul in Jerusalem, Victor Beauboucher. A Frenchman, wounded fighting for the Union in the Civil War, Beauboucher was the only Jerusalem consul in American history who was not himself a U.S. citizen. He had made himself exceedingly unpopular with Palestine's Jews when he utilized the power of his office to assist Protestant missionaries in their heavy-handed but ultimately unsuccessful attempt to entice a young Jewish orphan named Sarah Steinberg to take up the Protestant faith adopted by her closest relatives. Sneersohn, and many of the community's Jews, wanted him removed.[17]

Rabbi Haim Zvi Sneersohn

Sneersohn knew how to attract attention to his cause. Rather than dressing in traditional East European Hasidic clothing (which might have been exotic enough), he always appeared in public looking "very imposing and venerable" bedecked in an "Oriental costume" consisting of a "rich robe of silk, a white damask surplice, a fez, and a splendid Persian shawl fastened about his waist." People paid to see a man like that lecture in English. His addresses attracted Jews and Christians alike.[18]

Arriving in Washington, Sneersohn lectured twice on Jews in the Holy Land, with "members of the President's family . . . and of Congress" in attendance. He also met with the secretary of state to talk about the Jerusalem consulate. Then, on April 20, just weeks after the inauguration, he called upon President Grant in the White House, barging in, according to a widely reprinted account from Washington's *National Intelligencer*, "on the informal reception given in his chair by the President to many whom he was favoring with a few words of private conversation." The president "rose courteously to receive the Rabbi," and Sneersohn responded with the traditional blessing for rulers: "Blessed are You, Lord our God,

King of the Universe who has given of His glory to human beings." He then carried out his mission, imploring Grant "to turn your attention to the deplorable condition of my brethren in the Orient, that the principles of the Government may be truly embodied in its representatives abroad"—a long-winded way of asking him to replace Beauboucher (who, unbeknownst to him, was ailing and seeking transfer to "a post in Italy, Spain or Germany"). He also asked Grant to "enable my brethren in the Holy Land in the hour of need to seek refuge under the Stars and Stripes." The president, described as "deeply moved by the Rabbi's sincere and feeling words," asked several questions and then, in his characteristically laconic way, announced, "I shall look into this matter with care." Sneersohn, in response, offered a "fervent prayer" for Grant and his family, and departed. At least so far as the *National Intelligencer* was concerned, he had succeeded in his mission. "The American Government can not refuse so humble a request," the newspaper concluded. "[T]he Israelites . . . shall have in the American consulate at Jerusalem an advocate."[19]

Sneersohn, having accomplished his mission and become something of a media sensation, proceeded across the United States, lecturing and attracting notice wherever he went. By the time news of the Romanian atrocities burst into the press, he had reached San Francisco, taking advantage of the then newly completed transcontinental railroad, which, within a decade, would transform that city into the second-largest Jewish community in the United States. His host and companion in San Francisco was Benjamin Franklin Peixotto, scion of a distinguished Sephardic family, a lawyer, journalist, and exceptional orator who had studied under the guidance of Stephen A. Douglas, had served as political editor of the Cleveland *Plain Dealer*, and (not least important) was a boyhood friend of Simon Wolf. Peixotto, at thirty-five, was the same age as the rabbi and had already accumulated a distinguished record of communal activism as national president ("Grand Saar") of B'nai B'rith, leader of Tifereth Israel Congregation, and founder of the pioneering Cleveland Jewish Orphan

Benjamin Franklin Peixotto

Home. Now, under Sneersohn's careful prodding, he decided to become his people's savior as well.[20]

"I am ready and willing to go to Bucharest," Peixotto announced in a dramatic letter, putting forth his own name for the consulship that had been all but promised to Adolphe Buchner. He understood that the position carried no salary. He himself would have to raise whatever funds he needed. He also understood that the situation for Romania's Jews was not nearly so dire as the sensational press had first reported. Much to the embarrassment of American Jewish leaders, reports of large-scale massacres had turned out to be greatly exaggerated. But Romanian Jews remained deeply oppressed ("their property and lives treated as so much paper"), and Sneersohn had persuaded Peixotto to make the plight of "our poor unhappy people" his mission. "Heaven," the would-be consul piously avowed, "hath not placed it in my power to show the extent of the sacrifice I would make for suffering humanity, for persecuted Israel." His goal, as he prepared to offer that sacrifice, was twofold: to "revolution[ize] the social and religious life of our people" and to "effectually secur[e] their civil and political rights." Abraham Seligman (brother of Joseph and Jesse) supported his plan, he reported, and he expected that the Seligman brothers would also help to fund it. As for Buchner, Peixotto had it on the high authority of Rabbi Sneersohn ("my constant companion and counsellor") that he was "in no way fitted and must not be confirmed."[21]

Earlier, Sneersohn had himself written directly to President Grant about Romania ("have compassion upon five hundred thousand creatures of God left to the bloodiest ruthlessness—the most cruel harshness"). Never wanting in self-confidence, the rabbi urged the appointment of "a Jewish citizen . . . as Consul," a slap at Buchner, who, like Sneersohn's nemesis, Consul Beauboucher of Jerusalem, was not a citizen. "Such an example of so great and mighty a nation in its appreciation of men and its honor of their rights without regard to religious belief," he advised the president, "could not fail to make an impression." Peixotto, who was at once native-born, religiously engaged, and highly accomplished, was in Sneersohn's view the perfect choice. Although Simon Wolf was unimpressed by "the machinations of Rabbi Sneersohn" and considered the man "unpredictable and impracticable," and although Peixotto admitted to not having supported Grant in the 1868 election, Wolf "very reluctantly" sent his name to Grant and withdrew Buchner's. Grant obligingly forwarded the name to the Senate and, by unanimous consent, that body approved the nomination on June 29. Even Isaac Mayer Wise, long a critic of Grant, applauded this nomination. "Mr. Peixotto," he editorialized, "is the right man in the right place. He is able, zealous and patriotic. The thanks of the Hebrew citizens are due to President Grant for this judicious selection."[22]

Months passed while Peixotto wound up his affairs and raised funds for what was now called, as if it were a religious undertaking, his "mission." The wealthy Seligmans agreed to contribute or raise over $5,000 to enable the new consul, as Jesse Seligman contemptuously put it, "to make the trial for a couple of years with those benighted and semi-civilized heathens, our co-religionists in Romania." Jews who were less wealthy but more altruistic, B'nai B'rith members in particular, contributed, too. Like many a Protestant missionary, however, Peixotto through the years would be perennially short of money. Romanian Jewry's immense needs, coupled with those of his own large family, would regularly outstrip his all-too-meager means.[23]

In the meanwhile, on December 8, Peixotto traveled to Washington and, in the company of Simon Wolf, met with the president. Grant, both men later recalled, spoke unequivocally about human rights. He described "respect for human rights" as the "first duty of those set as rulers over nations" and specifically included both Blacks and Jews as being among the unfortunates whom "those in authority" should go out of their way to protect, "to rescue and redeem them and raise them up to equality with the most enlightened." As before, when he spoke out on behalf of Jews in Russia, so, too, now Grant paid no heed to those who urged silence concerning the internal affairs of other nations, nor did he consider America's foreign policy interests paramount. Instead, telling Jewish leaders just what they wanted to hear, he declared that "the story of the sufferings of the Hebrews of Roumania profoundly touches every sensibility of our nature. . . . It is one long series of outrage and wrong; and even if there be exaggeration in the accounts which have reached us, enough is evident to prove the imperative duty of all civilized nations to extend their moral aid in behalf of a people so unhappy."[24]

As if to underscore his commitment to human rights, as well as his atonement for past sins against the Jewish people, Grant subsequently wrote in his own hand (and without consulting his secretary of state) a letter of introduction for Peixotto that spelled out the unique nature of his mission:

EXECUTIVE MANSION

Washington Dec 8., 1870

The bearer of this letter Hon Benj F. Peixotto, who has accepted the important though unremunerative position of U.S. Consul-General to Roumania is commended to the good offices of all representatives of this government abroad.

Mr Peixotto has undertaken the duties of his present office more as a missionary work for the benefit of the people who are laboring under severe oppression than for any benefits to accrue to himself, a work which all good citizens will wish him the greatest success in. The United States knowing no distinction of her own citizens on account of religion or nativity naturally believe in a civilization the world over which will secure the same universal liberal views.

U. S. Grant[25]

Simon Wolf delivered this remarkable document to Peixotto and, sensing its significance, likewise provided a copy to the Associated Press—without, however, obtaining prior presidential permission. His intentions, like those of so many who leak government documents to the press, were (at least in his own mind) entirely for the good. He believed that the letter underscored America's solemn commitment to human rights the world over—for Jews no less than for Blacks. He considered it proof that Grant had learned the lesson of General Orders No. 11. He even, according to Peixotto, felt that publicizing the document "would make the name of General Grant immortal." All of these good intentions, however, counted for little in Washington. The misstep almost resulted in the revocation of Peixotto's appointment.[26]

Hamilton Fish was furious when he read the text of Grant's note in the newspaper. He had previously made clear to Peixotto that "he mistakes the object of his appointment" if his principal goal was to aid his fellow Jews, and he sternly informed him that as consul he had "no political functions or responsibilities." Having little sympathy with Grant's effort to inject human rights into American diplomacy, he now expressed to Wolf his "deep dis[s]atisfaction" with Peixotto. It was, he thought, an "indignity" that Peixotto had gone to Grant after Fish had refused him a "special letter" of introduction, and it was even worse that the extraordinary letter had now been published. Writing in his diary, Fish expressed a strong desire to "revoke his appointment."[27]

Wolf, whether out of base cowardice or clever duplicity, failed to confess his own role in obtaining and publishing Grant's note. Instead, he concurred with all that Fish complained about, and then persuaded the secretary not to revoke Peixotto's appointment. As a result, the document that Grant wrote was widely publicized and remains a pioneering statement on the role of human rights in American diplomacy, a signal achievement of Grant's presidency. By contrast, the objections that Fish articulated received no notice at all. Peixotto, meanwhile, set off for Romania.[28]

There, much as Rabbi Sneersohn had anticipated and Secretary of State Fish had feared, Peixotto devoted the bulk of his energies to improving the lot of the country's Jews. He strongly advocated for their emancipation and citizenship; promoted education and modernization; created and subsidized a pro-Jewish liberal newspaper; established a Jewish fraternal organization parallel to B'nai B'rith; and in 1872 took the lead in aiding the Jews of Ismail and surrounding communities who were viciously attacked and plundered after a Jewish apostate, who had robbed and defiled a church, was tortured into implicating wealthy Jews as abettors of his crime. Peixotto provided refuge in his own home for some of those attacked, and eventually won the release of all the innocents. In a private letter, he gave vent to his true feelings about Romania at that time: "The lightning of heaven," he wrote, "should blast a country so infamous."[29]

In response, Peixotto advocated large-scale Jewish emigration to the United States, an objective that Romania's antisemitic government, eager to be rid of its Jews, enthusiastically encouraged. He even contacted his old friend Governor Edward S. Salomon, who, as we have seen, was busy investing in land, about the possibility of settling Romanian Jews in the Washington Territory. Revealingly, Peixotto's plan closely echoed Grant's own thinking about how to empower persecuted minorities. In 1870, Grant had proposed acquiring Santo Domingo as an American protectorate, in part so that mistreated ex-slaves might immigrate there. His goal, as he later explained, was to make "the negro 'master of the situation,' by enabling him to demand his rights at home on pain of finding them else-where." Peixotto, in 1872, applied this same rationale with respect to Jews:

> Let 20,000 go to America & the report they will *send back* will bring 20,000 more. Then the Roumanians will do as the Egyptians did, they will cling to the skirts of the remainder and pray them with streaming eyes to abide *in the land of their birth*![30]

Emigration fever quickly spread among the poorer Jews of Romania. Peixotto's plan even spurred the publication of a Hebrew volume by journalist Leon Horowitz describing the wonders of America to poten-tial immigrants. Rabbi Isaac Mayer Wise in Cincinnati enthusiastically endorsed the idea: "Let them come, one and all, farmers, mechanics, arti[s]ans, young people willing and able to work; let them come one and all, we have plenty of room and bread for a few millions more." Several notable American newspapers, led by the *New York Herald*, agreed. But the plan also met with a barrage of criticism from those who both feared its costs and implications and doubted its feasibility. The Anglo-Jewish bar-rister and politician Sir Francis Goldsmid worried that it would "divert attention from the really important question, that of Jewish rights." A group of wealthy and privileged Romanian Jews complained that the plan made them appear unpatriotic. A distinguished gathering of Jewish lead-ers, meeting in Brussels, unanimously rejected the plan as "injudicious and inadvisable." Even Peixotto's erstwhile "constant companion and counsellor," Haim Zvi Sneersohn, attacked the plan. Since he thought that Romanian Jews should remove to the Holy Land to help spur resto-ration to Zion ("a Jewish independent commonwealth in the land of our forefathers"), the rabbi assailed the plan of his former protégé in what has been described as "biblical but ill-tempered invective."[31]*

---

* In 1874, Sneersohn himself returned to Tiberias in hopes of establishing a Jewish agricultural colony there. Jewish religious zealots in that city opposed his plan and excommunicated him. Subsequently, they physically attacked him, robbed him of his

By contrast, Hamilton Fish now had nothing but complimentary things to say about Peixotto, particularly his role in aiding persecuted Jews and building a diplomatic coalition in favor of human rights. The secretary of state enjoyed seeing other foreign consuls take their lead from an American, and heard good reports concerning Peixotto from a Russian diplomat whom he trusted. The idea that America, having cast slavery aside, might serve as a beacon of freedom to persecuted peoples had apparently grown on him. "I know you will be glad to learn that we have sustained Mr. Peixotto in all he has done and will continue to support him in whatever he does discreetly for the benefit of his Jewish friends," the secretary of state told a surprised Adolphus Solomons in 1872, in Grant's presence. Fish admitted that at first he found Peixotto "a little too enthusiastic" and "took him to task," but now, he repeated, "I am perfectly satisfied with all he has done." The president, Solomons reported, listened with evident interest to most of the conversation—a sure sign that Fish was speaking as much to him as to Solomons.[32]

Peixotto's adroit mixture of consular diplomacy and human rights advocacy during the five years and three months he spent in Romania (1870–1876) did not, in the end, secure full civil and religious rights for Jews. Nor did they revolutionize Jewish social and religious life in the country. Nor did they produce any plan for resettling thousands of Romanian Jews in the United States. But if his own goals went unrealized, Peixotto did abundantly fulfill Ulysses S. Grant's goals in appointing him. He engaged in "missionary work" for the benefit of Jews "laboring under severe oppression." He furthered the then novel idea in American diplomacy that the "United States knowing no distinction of her own citizens on account of religion or nativity naturally believe in a civilization

---

worldly possessions, stripped him stark naked, strapped him to the back of an ass, and paraded him through the streets and outside the city walls. To shocked onlookers, they explained that the rabbi was religiously delusional and considered himself to be the Messiah. Israel Klausner, *Rabbi Hayyim Zvi Sneersohn* (Jerusalem: Mosad Harav Kook, 1973), 108.

the world over which will secure the same universal liberal views." He articulated a vision of America as a proponent of universal freedom. And he powerfully symbolized the emergence of America's Jews on the world scene. The fact that a proud, publicly self-identifying, energetic, and somewhat brash "Israelite" represented the United States in Bucharest delivered the message to persecuted peoples everywhere that "America was different." Having internalized that message of hope, tens of thousands of Romanian Jews would immigrate to the United States in the twentieth century. At the same time, the Jewish consul likewise delivered the message that, as president, Ulysses S. Grant was different, a far cry from the general who had expelled "Jews as a class" back in 1862.

Whether other American Jews who had opposed Grant now accepted the idea that Grant was different remained to be seen. His reelection campaign, in 1872, looked to be a referendum on that question. It would show whether he had successfully redeemed himself with Jewish voters: whether his postelection apology ("I do not sustain that order"), his unprecedented number of Jewish appointments, his sensitivity to human rights for Jews abroad, and his remarkable letter to Benjamin F. Peixotto had persuaded them that he was now their friend and ally.

Democrats, seeking to prevent any such alliance, naturally reminded Jews of General Orders No. 11 ("that infamous order banishing the Jews as a class from his district because, forsooth, a few of them were petty traders"). An anti-Grant cartoon even offered up a visual reminder of the order. Produced by Matt Morgan, chief cartoonist for *Leslie's Illustrated*, it recalled a famous scene from Shakespeare's *The Merchant of Venice*, where Shylock, depicted by Morgan as a bareheaded, noble, and oddly sympathetic Jew, explained to Antonio, the stony-faced and obdurate Ulysses S. Grant, why, having insulted him in the past, he now had no claim upon him for help. A copy of General Orders No. 11, posted on the wall, reminded readers just what those past insults were. The cartoon encouraged latter-day Jews to respond to Grant on Election Day just as (the noble) Shylock had once responded to Antonio: by recalling the insult

Matt Morgan's cartoon "Then and Now" carried a caption from *The Merchant of Venice* with Shylock, in this case, declaiming his words to Grant: "You call me misbeliever, cut-throat dog, And spit upon my Jewish gaberdine, And all for use of that which is mine own. Well then, it now appears you need my help."

and wreaking revenge. So balanced a portrait of Shylock—implying that Democratic voters should side with him—was quite remarkable for its time and signaled that Americans viewed Jews far more positively in 1872 than they had a decade earlier. It may also have served to tacitly critique the pro-Grant cartoonist Thomas Nast, who had earlier employed the same scene from *The Merchant of Venice* to attack August Belmont as a "Shylock" for supplying money and votes to the Democrats. But would Jews really ally themselves with "the party of Shylock" to vote against Grant's reelection?[33]

To encourage them, Isaac Mayer Wise dredged up the fact that back in 1861 the new vice president on Grant's Republican ticket, Senator Henry Wilson, had condemned Louisiana's Jewish senator, Judah P. Benjamin, as "the son of that race which stoned the prophets and crucified the Redeemer of the world." He failed to mention that the Democratic candidate for the vice presidency, Missouri's B. Gratz Brown, had supported the "religious amendment" to the Constitution. Other Democrats recycled anti-Grant propaganda from the 1868 election campaign. But in the end, none of this carried much weight with Jewish voters. Even Wise admitted that Grant had "made sufficient atonement" for General Orders No. 11, and that "we have long ago forgiven him that blunder." The *Jewish Messenger* observed that other Jews had likewise forgiven him, burying "their private feelings in consideration of the eminent public services of the General." The *Hebrew Leader* went so far as to publish a long adulatory article on Grant, concluding that he was entitled to "the gratitude and respect of the Jewish-American citizens." Even Jewish voters in the South, who had united against Grant four years earlier, now expressed themselves in his favor. A straw poll of fifty-three Southern Jewish delegates to a B'nai B'rith convention found forty-five Grant supporters and only eight supporters of his opponent, newspaperman Horace Greeley.[34]

In the end, of course, Grant won reelection by a landslide. His victory—the largest, in percentage terms, for any candidate between Andrew Jackson in 1828 and Theodore Roosevelt in 1904—was mostly due to his domestic and foreign policy successes coupled with Greeley's comically poor showing on the stump (one observer characterized Greeley as "so conceited, fussy and foolish that he damages every case he wants to support"). Still, when Grant subsequently expressed satisfaction "that the people had vindicated his private character," he might also have had the Jewish people in mind. Over the course of four years, he had largely won them over. In doing so, primarily through his sensitivity to minority rights at home and human rights abroad, he helped to clarify his own presidential vision. The American values that he now trumpeted were values that Jews held exceedingly dear.[35]

The next four years were something of an anticlimax. The landslide election made Republican politicians incautious, and, as so often happens in such cases, hubris bred maladministration, misconduct, corruption, and scandal. Men whom Grant trusted betrayed him. Journalists and critics had a field day. Jews joined in condemning "the corruption in official circles, which has largely corrupted all classes of society," but did not blame the president more than others in positions of power. They understood perfectly well that, in Isaac Mayer Wise's words, moral rot was no less pervasive among the "Democratic rulers of the city of New York" (Boss Tweed and Tammany Hall) than among "the national rulers in Washington." The call therefore went out to ordinary citizens to effect reform. "In spite of all the extraordinary exertions of men in power, in spite of threats, bribes, espionage and denunciation . . . there is no cause of apprehension," Wise reassured his readers. "This is a morally sound people."[36]

The presidential initiative that earned the most support from Jews during Grant's scandal-plagued second term was his effort to strengthen church-state separation. Protestant efforts to Christianize the country and the Catholic campaign to win state funding for parochial schools had come to alarm religious liberals, who favored the high wall of separation that Thomas Jefferson so famously advocated. Jews, newly accepted as insiders by the president, were particularly fearful of seeing their gains reversed. As a result, historian Benny Kraut has shown, a "natural, pragmatic alliance" developed, uniting "Jews, liberal Christians, religious free thinkers, and secularists in common bond, their religious and theological differences notwithstanding."[37] Members of this alliance sought to shift away from Abraham Lincoln's emphasis on Americans as a religious people, and toward a greater stress on government as a secular institution. Rabbi Max Lilienthal of Cincinnati, for example, elevated the separation of church and state into one of the central tenets of American Judaism:

> [W]e are going to lay our cornerstone with the sublime motto, "Eternal separation of state and church!" For this reason we shall never favor or ask any support for our various benevolent institutions by the state; and if offered, we should not only refuse, but reject it with scorn and indignation, for those measures are the first sophistical, well-premeditated steps for a future union of church and state. Sectarian institutions must be supported by their sectarian followers; the public purse and treasury dares not be filled, taxed and emptied for sectarian purposes.[38]

Grant probably knew nothing of Lilienthal (though the rabbi had written to him in 1871 seeking to have his son, Jesse, appointed to a cadetship at West Point).[39] In 1875, however, he threw his support behind a parallel vision of "strict separation," insisting that religion be kept out of the public schools and that state aid be denied to parochial schools. "Leave the matter of religion to the family altar, the church, and the private school supported entirely by private contribution," Grant declared in an address in Des Moines to veterans of the Army of the Tennessee, the soldiers he had led when General Orders No. 11 was issued. The central point of his speech, one of the most important that he ever delivered, was "keep the church and state forever separate." Subsequently, in his State of the Union message to Congress that year, Grant spoke out in favor of a constitutional amendment to require states to create free public schools for all children, "forbidding the teaching in said schools of religious, atheistic, or pagan tenets; and prohibiting the granting of any school funds or school taxes . . . for the benefit or in aid, directly or indirectly, of any religious sect or denomination."[40] Catholics and evangelicals were appalled, and some still charge him with secularism and anti-Catholicism; his amendment never won congressional approval. Jews who agreed with Grant, however, believed that his advocacy of this and related issues placed him "in the foremost rank of the statesmen of the Republic." They congratulated him for having the courage to raise questions "upon the solution of which at no distant day probably the perpetuity of free institutions depends."[41]

Having argued that religion belonged firmly at the family altar and the church, Grant accepted the invitation of his friend Adolphus Solomons to attend the June 9, 1876, dedication of Adas Israel, the first Jewish house of worship in Washington to be built specifically as a synagogue. Adas was the smaller and more modest of Washington's two Jewish congregations, and it was Orthodox. Simon Wolf and the bulk of the city's German-Jewish elite worshipped in the larger and more outwardly impressive Washington Hebrew Congregation, founded in 1852, whose shorter and more liberal services took place in a former Methodist church.

Grant made history by attending Adas Israel's dedication. No American president had ever attended a synagogue dedication before (although potentates of countries far less sympathetic to Jews had). Since the event was carefully timed to coincide with the celebration of one hundred years of American independence, the president's appearance was particularly laden with symbolism. It announced that Judaism was a coequal religion in the United States. Twenty years earlier, almost to the day, Congress had enacted special legislation to ensure that "all the rights, privileges, and immunities heretofore granted by law to the Christian churches in the city of Washington, be . . . extended to the Hebrew Congregation of said city." Now, the man who had once expelled "Jews as a class" from his war zone personally came to honor Jews for upholding and renewing their faith.[42]

The dedication, beginning at 4:00 p.m., lasted for three full hours.

Adas Israel Synagogue

Grant, his son Ulysses Jr., and the president pro tempore of the Senate, acting vice president Thomas W. Ferry of Michigan, surprised the congregation by remaining until the end. American flags draped each side of the ark, and "flowers whose fragrance filled every part of the place" made the heat seem less oppressive. Patriotism, dignity, and decorum characterized the dedication; a special synagogue ordinance went so far as to ban "loud praying" during the event (on other occasions, the synagogue's historian reports, such elevated standards of behavior "were seldom observed"). In a particularly "beautiful and impressive" ceremony, rarely seen before and much commented upon afterward, the synagogue's eternal lamp was lowered on a silver cord and lighted. George Jacobs of Philadelphia, the officiating Jewish "minister," then offered the requisite prayer "for the Government of the United States" and delivered a sermon linking the synagogue's dedication to America's centennial. When it was all over, the dignitaries in attendance responded generously. Senator Ferry, raised in the home of Presbyterian missionaries, commented that "he would gladly have waited another hour" had the sermon been further prolonged, "for much that was new was learned, and many prejudices removed." Grant handed in a subscription card promising the congregation $10 (worth about $200 in today's money), earning him its sincere thanks for his "munificence and liberality."[43]

One month later, Grant found himself in renewed contact with Jews.

The annual convention of the Council of the Union of American Hebrew Congregations, then a broad-based synagogue body established in 1873 to "preserve Judaism" and promote Jewish education, met in Washington to mark America's centennial. Grant set aside an hour to meet and greet them, and to show them the inside of the White House. One of those who introduced themselves to the president on the tour was Isaac Mayer Wise, a central figure in the organization. "I know all about you, Doctor," Grant was quoted as replying, "especially in connection with Order No. 11." Wise himself properly appreciated the larger significance of the gathering: "[Judaism's] existence as an element in this country has been made tangible and real to all by a representative body." The fact that Grant used the occasion to recall his Civil War order banishing Jews, however, serves as yet another reminder that whenever he found himself in Jews' company, the blot on his military record—the sense that in expelling "Jews as a class" he had failed to live up to his own high standard of what it meant to be an American—was never far from his mind.[44]

As it turned out, this was Ulysses S. Grant's last major engagement with Jews during his presidency. The following March, after steering the country through one of its tightest-ever presidential elections as well as multiple postelection challenges, he turned power over to Rutherford B. Hayes. With that, a brief "golden age" in the history of the American Jewish community came to an end. The Grant years had brought Jews heightened visibility in the United States and new levels of respect. More Jews served in public office than ever before, and America, for the first time, had firmly committed itself, even in its relations with other nations, to human rights policies, "making no distinction . . . on account of religion or nativity," with the aim of securing "universal liberal views."

Optimism suffused the American Jewish community at this time. A liberal Jewish magazine entitled, significantly, *The New Era* promised to "advance mankind in true religious knowledge and to unite all God's children in a common bond of brotherhood." A rabbi named Isidor Kalisch, speaking in "every important city east of the Mississippi River," confidently proclaimed the approach of "the golden age of a true universal brotherhood." City after city in the United States witnessed the construction of new synagogues, some of them, like Washington, D.C.'s Adas Israel, comparatively modest; others, like Rodeph Shalom in Philadelphia (1871) and Central Synagogue (Ahawath Chesed) in New York (1872), magnificently grand. The establishment of the Union of American Hebrew Congregations (1873), the first successful American synagogue organization, and of Hebrew Union College (1875), the first successful American rabbinical school, underscored the progress made by American Jews during the Grant years. Among themselves and in relating to their non-Jewish neighbors, Jews had seemingly internalized the president's watchword, "let us have peace."[45]

Clearly, Grant was not responsible for all of the progress that American Jews had made during his years in the White House. Nevertheless, his statements and actions, so starkly in contrast with what he had said and done during the Civil War, set a new national tone. Akin to the biblical seer Balaam, he had been expected to curse the Jews and ended up blessing them. Looking back some forty years later, Simon Wolf, while hardly a dispassionate observer, still recalled the Grant years as a unique era in American Jewish life. Having known every American president from James Buchanan to Woodrow Wilson, he concluded that "President Grant did more on behalf of American citizens of Jewish faith at home and abroad than all the Presidents of the United States prior thereto or since."[46]

6

"Then and Now"

Ulysses S. Grant left the White House on March 5, 1877. Ten weeks later, on May 17, he embarked on what became "perhaps the grandest tour an American couple had ever made." The general had always loved to travel. Now, at age fifty-five, he took advantage of the wondrous improvements in transportation made possible by the steam engine, as well as the fabulous profits yielded by his successful investment in twenty-five shares of Consolidated Virginia Mining, the company that extracted silver from the Comstock Lode, to set forth with his wife, his son Jesse, and a small entourage upon a trip around the world. It lasted for almost a thousand days.[1]

Several stops on the widely publicized journey proved of especial interest to Jews. When Grant arrived in Frankfurt, for example, one of those greeting him was his friend Henry Seligman. The short, stout, kindly entrepreneur, who was then running the Frankfurt branch of the family banking empire, had first befriended Grant back in 1848 in Watertown, New York, when the Seligmans were still in the dry goods business. Now, as one of the most powerful Jews in Frankfurt, he gallantly proposed a toast to "the health of General Grant," eliciting a warm reply from his old friend thanking the entire German city for the confidence it placed in the Union during the Civil War. Later, in Paris, other members of the far-flung Seligman banking family likewise appeared at the station to greet and fete the former president. The Seligmans always believed in looking out for their friends, and had particularly good reason to do so in Grant's case. They knew that as president he had directed substantial business in their direction. Moreover, in 1869, he had broadly hinted to the brothers that it would be advisable "to disassociate themselves" from banker Jay Gould, who was attempting to corner the market in gold, leading its price to skyrocket. When, on "Black Friday" (September 24, 1869), the price of gold as well as the stock market as a whole collapsed following unexpected government intervention, the Seligmans had made their money and "were entirely out of the market." Most other bankers, as well as hordes of speculators, had not been nearly so fortunate.[2]

After he left the White House, Grant maintained his friendship with the Seligmans. Indeed, according to Grant's onetime aide-de-camp Adam Badeau, he not only enjoyed the company of his "Jewish friends" but was "quite as much at home with the Seligmans as if they had been princes." This was especially significant since, less than a month before the Grants and the Seligmans fraternized in Frankfurt, Joseph Seligman, in New York, had traveled to Saratoga's Grand Union Hotel and been abruptly turned away at the door. Judge Henry Hilton, the Grand Union's new owner, had given strict instructions that "no Israelites shall be permitted in future to stop at this hotel." The calculated insult avenged an earlier clash between Seligman and Hilton, drew a sharp response from Seligman ("a little reflection must show to you that the serious falling off in your business is not due to the patronage of any one nationality, but to want of the patronage of all, and that you, dear Judge, are not big enough to keep a hotel"), and outraged public opinion. But it proved an ominous portent of social trends.[3]

Within a few years, "Jews as a class"—the same phrase Grant had used back in 1862—were declared unwelcome even at New York's Coney Island, and social discrimination against Jews became commonplace across the country. A short-lived American Society for the Suppression of the Jews, established in 1879, pledged its members, among other things, not to elect Jews to public office, not to attend theaters where Jewish composers wrote the music or Jewish actors performed, not to buy or read

Puck caricatures the Grand Union Hotel's antisemitic policies (1877).

books by Jewish authors, not to ride on Jewish-owned railroads, and not to do business with Jewish-owned insurance companies. Just as African Americans, in the years following Grant's presidency, experienced the rise of discriminatory Jim Crow legislation and a tragic reversal of all the gains they had made during Reconstruction's heyday, so, albeit not nearly to the same extent, the social status of Jews likewise declined. "The highest social element," Coney Island developer Austin Corbin explained, "won't associate with Jews, and that's all there is about it." Against this background, Grant's ongoing friendship with the Seligmans made a bold public statement. Others might discriminate against "Jews as a class," but Grant, in his later years, interacted with them comfortably.[4]

Grant interacted with Jews again when his tour reached the Holy Land. Visits by Americans to the land then known as Palestine were becoming more and more common at that time, part of what one author describes as "Holy Land mania." William Henry Seward, secretary of state under presidents Lincoln and Johnson, arrived in 1869; Grant's friend William Tecumseh Sherman in 1872. Earlier, in 1867, Samuel Clemens (Mark Twain) had made the trip aboard the steamer *Quaker City* and memorialized his experiences in *Innocents Abroad*, which Grant (like thousands of other travelers) took with him to read on the way. The great writer had found little to praise in the land that would one day become modern Israel. He described it as "monotonous and uninviting . . . a hopeless, dreary, heart-broken land." Even Jerusalem, in his eyes, was "mournful, and . . . lifeless." Religious pilgrims might romanticize the land of the Bible, but Mark Twain sought to puncture its halo. He was *"glad* to get away."[5]

Grant, the first American president ever to set foot on Jerusalem's holy soil, privately agreed with Mark Twain. "Our visit to Jerusalem was a very unpleasant one," he confided to Adam Badeau. "The roads are bad and it rained, blew and snowed all the time. We left snow six inches deep in Jerusalem." Journalist James Russell Young, who accompanied Grant and authored the best-known account of his journey, recalled that "from

General Grant and his wife in the Middle East

the time of landing until we left there was rain and snow—the heaviest snowstorm that had been known in Jerusalem for twelve years." To avoid alienating pious readers, however, Young and all of the others who produced books about Grant's round-the-world tour, glossed over these negative experiences and sentiments in their published accounts. They emphasized instead the country's exotic and sacred sights.[6]

That, in a sense, is just what Grant did. Rather than be diverted by the poor weather, he maintained his pace and visited as many holy sites as he could. In Jaffa, which he described, amusingly, as the place "where Jonah was swallowed by the whale," he and his wife marched through "one of the dirtiest streets in the world" and visited the reputed home of Simon the Tanner, the friend of Peter mentioned in the book of Acts. In Jerusalem, they hastened to the Via Dolorosa, "deeply interested," as Julia Grant put it, "to visit the places so familiar to us and so full of sacred import." In the Garden of Gethsemane, they pressed the knotted bark of "the Tree of Agony," and according to an accompanying journalist, "all thoughts turned to the sacred and sorrowful scenes which Christian men believe here took place."[7]

America's vice consul, Ernest Hardegg, a German Templar, accompanied Grant on his tour, and at his suggestion the party hired Rolla Floyd, a follower of the American religious enthusiast George J. Adams (both of them associated with the Reorganized Church of Jesus Christ of Latter-Day Saints), to guide them through Jerusalem. Hardegg and Floyd had come to Palestine fired with the dream of colonizing the Holy Land to spur the millennium, and their intense religious convictions shaped the tour that they devised. "Your thorough knowledge of Bible references, History & Tradition of all points of interest in the Holy Land and your clear and concise explanation of the same," Grant wrote in a thank-you note to Floyd, "has very much added to the interest and pleasure of our visit."[8]

Rabbi Haim Zvi Sneersohn tried to add his bit to the pleasure of Grant's visit as well. He met with Grant at the governor's residence and, predictably, offered him a heartfelt blessing. Probably at his initiative, a "committee for distributing relief to American Jewish citizens" in the Holy Land likewise held a meeting with the former president. "The deplorable condition of our community was made known to the General," Sneersohn reported to the *New York Herald*. Since the one hundred or so American Jews in the country were not formerly organized into an independent community (*kollel*), they received no funds from the central Jewish Vaad Ha-Klali charity fund, and were both poorer and more degraded than their European counterparts. They hoped that Grant would aid them in their battle to gain their fair share of communal distributions of aid. The general, having listened patiently, "kindly promised to inform some of his friends, leaders of Israel in America, of the facts." Whether he actually understood the "facts" concerning the convoluted politics of Jewish philanthropy in the land of Israel seems doubtful, nor is there any evidence that he followed through on his promise. Nevertheless, the publication in the *New York Herald* of this story, with its mention of Grant's friendship with "leaders of Israel in America," was significant. It underscored the image of himself that the former president strove mightily to cultivate.[9]

An anecdote preserved by Simon Wolf looked to reinforce that image. While in Jerusalem, according to Wolf, Grant was greeted by an unnamed Jew who "prostrated himself before him, kissing his hand." Years earlier this same man had written to Wolf in Yiddish requesting that he go to see the "King of the United States" and "bring to his attention the fact that he, the Jew of Jerusalem, had a daughter whom he wished to be married." In the best tradition of a Jerusalem schnorrer (distinguished from an ordinary beggar by his limitless chutzpah), the man had offered America's "king" "the honor" to contribute to his daughter's dowry. Grant, upon learning of this unusual request, wrote out a check for $25—equivalent to more than $400 in today's money.* In gratitude, according to Wolf, the

---

* Grant, according to Hamilton Fish, "gave to all who asked of him, giving from five to ten times the amounts that the applicants could have reasonably or probably expected." Hamilton Fish, interview, *The Independent*, July 30, 1885, as quoted in Smith, *Grant*, 607.

schnorrer now personally appeared before the former president in Jerusalem, "near the walls where the pious Jew offers his prayers," and fell at his feet. To be sure, published accounts of Grant's tour make no mention of this incident, which surely would have made for good journalistic copy. But even if Wolf embellished his account, it conveyed the same central message that Grant's meeting with Rabbi Sneersohn and so many of his other encounters with Jews did—a reassuring message of friendship and generosity toward Jews in America, the Holy Land, and everywhere else in the world.[10]

Grant returned from his historic trip late in 1879. His journey, one writer gushed, was "the most remarkable ever made by any human being" and "one of the most important events of Modern History." He returned from it as something of a world statesman, commanding an international following. As a result, friends urged him to seek the presidency again in 1880, building upon his new status as a global celebrity. "I am not a candidate for any office," Grant replied, "nor would I hold one that required any manoeuvring or sacrifice to obtain." While this did not prevent his name from being entered into nomination, his unwillingness to appear at the convention or to further his candidacy in a public way doomed his chances of victory. After leading the voting through thirty-five contested ballots, he lost to James Garfield on ballot number thirty-six.[11]

Thanks to wealthy friends, Grant at age fifty-eight returned to private life, settling into a handsome brownstone in New York City. With help from the Seligmans, he entered the field of investment banking, joining his son as a silent partner in the firm of Grant and Ward, managed by the young Ferdinand Ward, known in his day as the "Napoleon of Wall Street." With Grant's illustrious name and Ward's illustrious reputation, the firm quickly succeeded. On paper, at least, Grant became rich.[12]

The new wealth, however, did not dim Grant's humanitarian instincts. The attention of the country, and especially of American Jews, was at that time focused upon Russia. The assassination there of Tsar Alexander II in 1881 sparked an orgy of anti-Jewish violence. Some 169 Jewish communities were attacked, twenty thousand homes destroyed, and tens of thousands of Jews economically ruined. New York Jews clamored for action to help their brethren abroad, and according to the *Jewish Messenger*, "U. S. Grant was the first to sign the call for a public meeting of citizens of New York." Grant, as part of his world tour, had visited both with the subsequently murdered tsar and with the son who succeeded him, and came away convinced that "the Russian empire was one of the worst governed in the world." Now, in keeping with the human rights policies that he articulated as president, he signed his name atop a call urging his fellow citizens, "without distinction of creed," to meet at New York's Chickering Hall "for the purpose of expressing their sympathy with the persecuted Hebrews in the Russian Empire." His endorsement helped make the public meeting held on February 1, 1882, a rousing success.[13]

Although Grant himself did not attend the meeting, "many persons of the highest social and intellectual status" in the city did. New York's mayor, puffed up for the occasion as "the chief magistrate of the greatest City in the Western world," chaired the proceedings. According to the *New York Times*, which devoted extensive coverage to the event, one speaker, Reverend Dr. John P. Newman, described Grant as being one of "three names associated with this mass-meeting that would have great influence with the Russian authorities." So significant, indeed, was Grant's association with the event that "many persons having the erroneous idea that Gen[eral] Grant was present, lingered for a moment or two [after the meeting closed], and repeated calls for 'Grant' were uttered." While those calls "received no response," Grant's connection with the meeting was preserved both in a widely circulated commemorative pamphlet and in the *Jewish Encyclopedia*. Meanwhile, the satirical journal *Puck* published a cartoon critical of Grant, accusing him of shameless hypocrisy. Recalling General Orders No. 11, which the general could never live down, it portrayed him shedding crocodile tears over the persecution of Jews in Russia while pandering toward the Jewish vote in the 1884 presidential election.[14]

THEN AND NOW.—1862 AND 1882.

"OH, NOW YOU WEEP, AND I PERCEIVE YOU FEEL
THE DINT OF PITY. THESE ARE GRACIOUS DROPS."

Grant shedding crocodile tears over the
persecution of Jews in Russia. The quote is from
Shakespeare's *Julius Caesar*, act 3, scene 3.

By the time the 1884 election rolled around, however, Grant was desti-
tute and largely out of politics. His business partner, Ferdinand Ward, the
Bernard Madoff–like swindler of his day, borrowed against securities, paid
out inflated dividends, used funds from one investor to pay off another,
and, inevitably, proved unable to cover his debts. At that point, the bubble
burst and the firm of Grant and Ward went bankrupt. Grant's entire net
worth, along with that of much of his family, vanished into thin air.

Soon afterward, in 1885, just as Grant was busy writing his Civil War
memoirs so as to provide for his family, he was struck down by cancer.
An iron will sustained him as his health deteriorated. He spent hours
writing and dictating, determined to finish his narrative. Meanwhile,
messages from around the country flowed into the Grant home wishing

the general well in his illness. On April 13, "the Rabbis of New York and adjacent States" conveyed their "sympathy to the stricken household" and offered prayers "to the Father of all to send strength to the sufferer to enable him to fight this great battle with the heroism worthy of so great a soldier." Subsequently, the council of the Union of American Hebrew Congregations extended its "heartfelt sympathy and best wishes for his early restoration to health." At least one rabbi, Edward Benjamin Morris Browne of Congregation Gates of Hope in New York, personally visited with Grant at his home.[15]

Grant took great pride in these expressions of sympathy from people of different faiths. "The [P]rotestant, the Catholic, and the Jew appointed days for universal prayer in my behalf," he boasted in a letter to his eldest son. In response to a Catholic priest who wished him well, he again expressed great pleasure in the fact that "Catholics, Protestants, and Jews, and all the good people of the Nation, of all politics as well as religions, and all nationalities seem to have united in wishing or praying for my improvement." That he explicitly included Jews in these letters, written just weeks prior to his death and decades before such expressions of religious inclusiveness had become commonplace, bespeaks the transformation that he had undergone since his Civil War days. In the heat of battle, as generals so often do, he had submerged individuals, focusing instead on armies and military objectives and categories of people, Jews among them. In the interim, remorseful over his wartime order expelling "Jews as a class" from his war zone, he had become a champion of racial and religious inclusiveness at home and human rights abroad. One of his longtime colleagues, General Adam Badeau, went so far as to describe him in the final sentence of a memoir tracing Grant's career from "Appomattox to Mount McGregor" as "the foremost representative of the rights of the individual man."[16]

Mount McGregor in the Adirondacks was the place where, thanks to the generosity of banker Joseph W. Drexel and his family, who made available their commodious summer cottage, Grant spent his final days. By then he was unable to speak and communicated largely through written notes. He spent most of his time in bed. On the morning of Thursday, July 23, 1885, his heroic struggle came to its sad but inevitable end. He was pronounced dead at 8:08 a.m.

News of the death spread quickly. "None will mourn his loss more sincerely than the Hebrew," the Philadelphia *Jewish Record* declared in its Friday edition, "and tomorrow in every Jewish synagogue and temple in the land the sad event will be solemnly commemorated with fitting eulogy and prayer."[17] "Tomorrow," the Saturday following Grant's demise, coincided with what is known in the Jewish calendar as *Shabbat Naḥamu*, the "Sabbath of Consolation." It follows the fast of the ninth of Av commemorating the destruction of the Temple. The prophetic reading set aside for that day, from Isaiah 40, begins, "Comfort ye, comfort ye O my people." Many a rabbinic sermon in Grant's memory opened with that text.

"Comfort ye, comfort ye O my people saith the Lord," Reverend Joseph Hayim Mendes Chumaceiro of Isaac Leeser's old congregation, Beth El Emeth in Philadelphia, sang out. He eulogized General Grant as God's "anointed messenger to wipe out the crime of ages from your sacred institutions so that slavery might be blotted out from this fair land forever." Opening with the same biblical text, Rabbi Isaac Mayer Wise, once a sworn enemy of Grant's, declared that "the whole nation stands in need of consolation." He credited Grant with saving "his country for its own sake, without any selfish thirst after fame and self-aggrandizement" and concluded that in the history of humanity, Grant's name stood "high above Caesar and Napoleon." Rabbi Benjamin Szold of Baltimore, who also preached on consolation, predicted that volumes would in time "be devoted to the great work of [Grant's] life, and posterity will ever revere in him the man who rescued a nation from the abyss of war and contention, and who having won glory and fame in war, aimed only at securing peace. His memory will remain among us as a blessing forever."[18*]

---

* Another sign of late-nineteenth-century Jews' strong attachment to Grant is the tradition that he was moved by Aaron Z. Friedman's *Tub Taam; or, Vindication of the Isra-*

Just as the rabbis were eulogizing Grant and preaching consolation, word was received from England of the passing (at age one hundred) of Sir Moses Montefiore, the most famous Jew in the world at that time and a leading Jewish philanthropist and public figure. His death, coming just five days after Grant's, inevitably called forth comparisons. Such would have been unimaginable two decades earlier, when Montefiore was revered and Grant reviled, but now joint commemorations took place. "Grant conquered with the sword, Montefiore with the gentle weapons of peace," Alfred Jones of the *Jewish Record* declared in Atlantic City. "Both were of worldwide fame, yet both singularly free from pride. . . . Both men died with the work of their lives fully performed." Moses Klein, writing from Philadelphia in the European Hebrew journal *Hamagid*, found a "wonderful similarity" between the two men: "The first fought with the sword for the freedom of thousands of slaves; the other with the arrows of his tongue for the freedom of a nation; in the first, we see the picture of 'stern justice,' in the other that of 'sweet charity'; the name of the first will go down the ages as a man of war, and that of the second as the old philanthropist." Yet, as the editor of the *Jewish Messenger* insisted, both heroes shared similar characteristics. They were "men of profound religious convictions, resolute in action, firm in their respective lives of duty; men who knew not fear [and] achieved success; men who alike drew strength and inspiration from the same Providence." At Covenant Hall in

---

elitish Way of Killing Animals (1876) "to eat only ritually slaughtered meat in the latter part of his life." There is no evidence either in Grant's published papers or in his wife's memoir that he insisted upon eating only kosher meat, or had even read Friedman's book, but one biographer does report that "throughout life the only meat he would eat was beef cooked to a cinder, for the sight of blood destroyed his appetite." Since kosher meat is drained and salted to remove all traces of blood, Grant's aversion to the sight of blood may be the source of this tradition. Joakim Isaacs, "Candidate Grant and the Jews," in *Jews and the Civil War: A Reader*, ed. Jonathan D. Sarna and Adam Mendelsohn (New York: New York University Press, 2010), 409n25; J. F. C. Fuller, *Grant and Lee: A Study in Personality and Generalship* (Bloomington: Indiana University Press, 1957), 64.

Philadelphia and at an Orthodox synagogue in Wilmington, portraits of Montefiore and Grant hung side by side.[19]

In reality, of course, Montefiore and Grant differed strikingly in their approaches to Jewish problems. Montefiore, spurred by traditional Jewish religious teachings, promoted Jewish rights around the world, made repeated visits to Zion, and passionately believed that "Palestine must belong to the Jews." Grant reached out to Jews from a sense of guilt, promoted human rights as an extension of his national vision, found Zion "unpleasant," and assumed that if a foreign country (like Romania) failed to grant Jews equal rights, they would find refuge in America. Each man spoke the language of human rights, but each did so from different motivations. Montefiore drew upon a religious tradition that shaped humanitarian politics in England. Grant drew upon a liberal tradition that held up the United States as an object lesson for the world. The two men, moreover, propounded opposing solutions to the problems of world Jewry: the one centered on the Promised Land (Zion), the other on the Golden Land (America). In the twentieth century, Jews would debate these issues lustily, ultimately voting with their feet on where to settle. But in 1885, both of these deceased heroes were simultaneously idolized. In city after city, Isaac Mayer Wise retrospectively observed, Jews "gloried in the idea that Moses Montefiore was a Jew and General Grant one of their fellow citizens."[20]

A few rabbis did courageously note blemishes on Grant's record. Sabato Morais delicately observed that the general's "brilliant qualities" had "partly been dimmed by ill-advised actions." Wise, with typical bluntness, recalled "the notorious order No. II, which President Lincoln characterized as an 'absurdity,' and General Grant himself called in aftertimes 'a foolish piece of business.'" Reverend Elias Eppstein of Adath Jeshurun in Philadelphia likewise addressed Grant's anti-Jewish order. For the most part, though, rabbis, like their ministerial and secular colleagues, focused upon Grant's virtues and achievements. Indeed, a great many synagogues (including Wise's) recited the traditional Jewish mourner's kaddish in the former president's memory. "Seldom before," the *Jewish Record* reported, "has the kaddish been repeated so universally for a non-Jew as in this case."[21]

The Jewish address that received the greatest nationwide attention was delivered by the rabbi who visited with Grant during his illness, Edward Benjamin Morris Browne. A Hungarian who immigrated to the United States in 1865, Browne was fluent in six languages and, alongside rabbinic ordination, boasted degrees in law and medicine. Since he proudly displayed all of his degrees after his signature—E. B. M. Browne, L.L.D, A.M., B.M., D.D., M.D.—he became known as Alphabet Browne. His difficult personality and self-centered conceit, compounded by health problems, impeded his career. He bounced from pulpit to pulpit—fifteen of them in a career that spanned half a century.[22]

Back in 1871, when he was all of twenty-six years old, Browne had recommended himself to Grant as chaplain to West Point Military Academy. Episcopalians and Methodists were publicly vying for that position, so Browne put his own name forward as a compromise candidate ("it seems to me that the Jews have perhaps more just claims . . . because no Jewish minister has yet been given a single office while the Christian clergy is very well represented in the offices of the U.S."). He was not seriously considered.[23]

Four years later, Illinois senator Richard J. Oglesby, who had served under Grant in the Civil War, recommended Browne for a small remunerative government position on the basis of his "high scholarly and literary attainments" and his "disease of the eyes." Browne met with Grant at that time, and later published what he claimed was an interview with the president in which, among other things, he quoted Grant as saying that "the Jew lives longer because he loves his life more," takes fewer risks than non-Jews, and is therefore rarely injured in railroad accidents, that Jewish soldiers were nevertheless "wonderfully courageous," and that he had "intimate friends among the Jews." Grant approved a minor consulate appointment for Browne ("If there is a South American consulate Mr. Browne can have, I have no objection to his appointment"), but none proved sufficiently remunerative and no appointment was made. Still, Browne kept up ties with Grant, and, according to his great-granddaughter, visited with him occasionally after he left office.[24]

On the Sabbath following Grant's death, Browne announced to his small New York congregation that "the Jews have lost a great friend in the death of Gen. Grant." He then proclaimed that it was time to "speak the whole truth" concerning General Orders No. 11. Grant, he disclosed, had made a confession to his Methodist minister, the Reverend Dr. John Philip Newman, in which he said the following: "I consider it now my duty to make known a secret that I have kept these twenty years and locate the responsibility upon the proper parties that have come to me from Washington direct. I protested against it, but had to promulgate it against my will. I shall make this statement in my book likewise." Newman, Browne said, had so informed his own family, and apparently confided in his friend Browne as well. Having revealed the "secret" to his congregants, Browne went on to deliver a stirring eulogy suggesting that Grant was even greater than Moses: "Moses liberated 3,000,000 of people, his own brethren, from Egyptian bondage. Grant liberated 3,000,000 of people, a race not his own, from American bondage." At the conclusion of his address, he instructed his entire congregation to rise and recite the mourner's kaddish in Grant's memory. "This is a prayer," he declared with typical exaggeration, "never recited for a non-Jew before." Thanks to wire services, the sensational story was reprinted around the country and Browne for a time became a celebrity.[25]

In fact, Browne's story does not bear close scrutiny. The rabbi himself, just a few years earlier, had quoted Grant in a personal interview as taking full responsibility for General Orders No. 11. Grant at that time explained that "there were army followers among us. It happened one day that a number of complaints reached me and in each case it was a Jew and I gave the order excusing the Jewish traders . . . it was no ill-feeling or want of good-feeling toward the Jews. If such complaints would have been lodged against a dozen men each of whom wore a white cravat, a black broadcloth suit, beaver or gold spectacles, I should probably have issued a similar order against men so dressed." Moreover, contrary to Browne, Grant made no mention at all of General Orders No. 11 in his memoirs. His son Frederick, we have seen, explained in his father's name that it "was a matter long past and best not referred to." Finally, as Edward Rosewater—editor of the *Omaha Bee* and a telegraph officer in the White House when General Orders No. 11 was issued—wrote in a sharp rebuttal, "Only three men in Washington had authority to issue orders to Gen. Grant": Abraham Lincoln, Edwin Stanton, and Henry Halleck. Rosewater testified that not one of the three had issued any such order, and labeled Browne an "impudent imposter."[26]

The Reverend Dr. John Philip Newman, in his own lengthy eulogy for Grant delivered at Mount McGregor on August 4, made a brief reference to General Orders No. 11 that seemed to echo what Browne had disclosed: "The order issued during the war, excluding certain Jewish traders from a given military district, did not originate with him," he declared, "but came from higher authority, and was not against the religion of the Jews." The *Jewish Messenger* properly criticized this as "perverting history," since Grant's order had excluded "Jews as a class," not "some Jewish traders," and "the order was his and not dictated by higher authority." It lamented, though, that the whole subject had been raised. "Contemporaries that refer to the 'Order No 11' incident in Grant's career—which none regretted more than he—are certainly ungracious," it complained. As for Newman, it submitted that as Grant's "eulogist and friend the reverend should have been silent on this subject."[27]

The fact that so many people during the period of Grant's death and funeral were far from "silent on the subject" underscores the importance of General Orders No. 11 for understanding Grant's career from 1862 onward. When General Grant expelled the Jews from his war zone, he raised questions about himself and about America's relationship to the Jews that shaped the remainder of his life. As president and even in his postpresidential years those questions repeatedly bobbed to the surface.

They colored all of his dealings with Jews, tainting his wartime record but also shaping his remarkable postwar record of support for Jews that lasted into the 1880s. Whenever he interacted with Jews, and especially when Jews suffered persecution, one senses that embarrassing memories of General Orders No. 11 flooded into his mind. Like other personal failings in his life, the mistake proved difficult for him to live down; he spent the rest of his life making amends for it.

Jews knew how much Grant regretted issuing his order. He had apologized for it publically and numbers of Jews had heard him lament it privately as well. Some of his non-Jewish friends also heard him regret what he had done. John M. Thayer, who knew Grant from the war onward and was appointed by him governor of the Wyoming Territory, recalled at the time of Grant's death that "Grant sincerely regretted having ever issued the order, and in conversation with him said it was a great mistake . . . it was a source of great regret to him that he had been instrumental in inflicting a wrong upon [the Jews]." Grant's wife, Julia, we have seen,

The funeral of President Ulysses S. Grant

likewise characterized the order against "Jews as a class" as "obnoxious." She knew that her husband felt guilty about ever having issued it.[28]

Those who planned Grant's funeral in New York, however, preferred Rabbi Browne's version of events absolving the general of all blame for the order. Notwithstanding burgeoning social antisemitism in America and the embrace of anti-Jewish hatred by some cultural and political leaders in Europe, they understood that America's greatest heroes were untainted by charges of religious prejudice. They wanted Grant purged of that taint as well. Perhaps for that reason, and likely at the instigation of John Newman, Browne was invited to serve as one of the fourteen honorary pallbearers at Grant's state funeral on August 8 in New York as representative of the entire Jewish community. The city's better-known rabbis, Reform and Orthodox alike, were all passed over (much to their annoyance), even as their counterparts among the city's foremost Protestant and Catholic clergy stood conspicuously among the honorees.[29]

August 8 was a Saturday, the Jewish Sabbath, and that posed a problem for Browne. The honorary pallbearers were scheduled to *ride* the seven-and-a-half-mile route of the funeral from City Hall to the vault in Riverside Park where Grant was to be buried. Riding on the Sabbath meant flouting Jewish law, which bars traveling in a carriage on the day of rest. Browne, as a Reform rabbi, had not always honored the Sabbath so punctiliously, but he considered it improper to publicly violate it as a representative of the Jewish community as a whole. Besides, he occupied the right wing of the Reform movement, being more traditional than Isaac Mayer Wise. His German immigrant congregation was likewise quite traditional—years later, indeed, it transformed itself into the Park Avenue Synagogue and joined the Conservative movement. So in a well-publicized bid to honor the Jewish Sabbath (and in a backhanded slap at Radical Reform rabbis who sought to shift the Jewish Sabbath to Sunday), Browne announced that "his religion forbade him to ride on the Sabbath . . . and it would be necessary for him to forgo attendance unless he were allowed to walk." The harried planners, who needed to worry

Rabbi E. B. M. ("Alphabet")
Browne, wearing his medals

about logistics for tens of thousands of people expected at the funeral, turned a deaf ear to this plea, but Browne went over their heads. "Since I cannot honor your sainted father and my religion both," he telegraphed Frederick Grant, he would "have to forego the honor." The Grant family promptly interceded—when it came to Jews it had every reason to be especially sensitive—and the decision was reversed. The *Daily Graphic* on August 8 carried the story just as Browne would have wanted it: "Rabbi Browne is 'footing it' to Riverside in honor of the Jewish Sabbath, and every time he sets foot upon the pavement he tramples upon the hearts of his opponents who tried to transfer the Jewish Sabbath to Sunday."[30]*

---

* The issue became an episode in a much larger debate in American Jewish life over the Jewish Sabbath, how to observe it, and whether it should be transferred to Sunday. Reform rabbis who cast off many proscriptions of Jewish law made fun of Browne, observing that even by walking such a long distance and carrying an umbrella, he was violating Jewish Sabbath restrictions. Orthodox rabbis, by contrast, presented

Original tomb of General Grant, Riverside Park, New York City, 1885

Having represented Jews at the funeral, Browne continued to honor Grant every year thereafter by journeying to "the tomb on Riverside Drive to place a wreath there." At the thirty-fifth memorial service, in 1920, he declared proudly: "Grant, we are here again." By then, he had styled himself "the oldest Minister in the American pulpit" and had lived long enough to become the last of Grant's pallbearers to annually appear at the tomb.[31]

The vault where Browne placed his wreath in 1920 was not the one in which Grant had originally been buried. Indeed, it required twelve years of planning, politicking, and fund-raising before Grant's remains were transferred into what is today known as Grant's Tomb. Opened on April 27,

Browne with a gold medal bearing the inscription *Boruch mekadesh HaShabos*— "blessed be he who sanctifies the Sabbath." *American Israelite* (August 14, 1885); Janice Rothschild Blumberg, "Voices for Justice: Rabbi Jacob M. Rothschild in Atlanta (1946–1973) and Edward B. M. Browne in New York (1881–1889)," online at http://spinner.cofc.edu/~jwst/pages/Blumberg,%20Janice%20-%20VOICES%20FOR%20JUSTICE%20++.pdf?referrer=webcluster& (accessed July 5, 2010).

1897, which would have been the general's seventy-fifth birthday, the tomb, according to scholars, was "rooted in the most substantial tradition of funerary memorials." Its prototype was said to be the mausoleum of the Roman emperor Hadrian, the Mausoleum Hadriani now known as the Castel Sant'Angelo (in Rome). From a Jewish perspective, that design could hardly have been less appropriate. Hadrian, after all, had been the Roman emperor who brutally put down the Jewish revolt against Rome (132–135 CE) led by Bar Kokhba. He murdered Jews by the thousands including eminent rabbis, restricted the study of the Torah and the practice of Judaism, and erected a gentile city (Aelia Capitolina) on the site of the destroyed city of Jerusalem. His name, in Jewish tradition, is followed by the imprecation "may his bones rot."[32]

Architect John Hemenway Duncan had no reason to know that, and Jews of the day, if they did know it, were silent. As a result, when Grant's Tomb was dedicated, Jews joined with fellow New Yorkers—about a mil-

Grant's Tomb, Riverside Drive, New York City, 1897

lion of them, it was estimated—to participate in and watch the grand celebration. Pittsburgh's Jewish newspaper listed by name ten local Jews from that city who journeyed to New York for the occasion. A huge "Grant parade," involving some fifty thousand marchers, included "pupils of the Hebrew Orphan Asylum, with their famous band," seventy-five "Alliance Cadets" representing the city's Hebrew Institute, and "many lads of Jewish parentage" from the public schools. This time, probably to the relief of the planners, General Orders No. 11 went unmentioned during the festivities. Instead, Rabbi Joseph Silverman of New York's Temple Emanu-El, the city's flagship Reform congregation, delivered a stirring sermon in advance of the event, taking as his text the "inscription over the door of the beautiful mausoleum," Grant's famous epigram "Let us have peace." He defended Grant against those who misunderstood him, labeled him "the Prince of Peace," and praised the new edifice as a "monument to his valor and greatness." Simon Wolf, in a piece printed in several Jewish newspapers, likewise offered a eulogistic tribute. "His tomb will stand on the banks of the Hudson," he concluded, "but his memory and achievements will live in the hearts of all men who love liberty and admire nobility of character for all time to come."[33]

Wolf, like so many other eulogists, proved much too optimistic. Though Grant was as popular as George Washington and Abraham Lincoln in the late nineteenth century, in the twentieth century his reputation fell under withering assault. Historians, many of them Southerners critical of his benevolent policy toward African Americans, criticized both the way he waged war and the way he forged peace. They blamed him for the Civil War's high death rate, for the failures of Reconstruction, for the corruption of his underlings, and for his personal failings. They derided him as a butcher and a drunkard. They ranked him close to the bottom among all American presidents: twenty-eighth out of twenty-nine presidents in 1948 (only Warren G. Harding ranked lower), and thirty-eighth out of forty-one in 1996.[34]

Jews joined in this outpouring of criticism. A standard work of American Jewish history by Rufus Learsi (Israel Goldberg), published in 1954, devoted three closely printed pages to Grant's General Orders No. 11 and barely a mention to the rest of his interactions with Jews. "Although Grant gave assurances that he regretted the Order," Learsi admonished, "those attempts at exculpation . . . were not convincing: the devil's tail of politics bulged out of them only too plainly." Two scholarly volumes on American antisemitism, published in 1994, reinforced the sense that the nation's eighteenth president was a hater of Jews. The *Encyclopaedia Judaica* confirms that in Jewish memory "Grant's name has been linked irrevocably with anti-Jewish prejudice."[35]

It is, of course, understandable why Jewish history should vilify a leader who blamed "Jews as a class" for the sins of smugglers and traders, and then expelled "Jews as a class" from the entire territory under his command. Yet Ulysses S. Grant deserved better. Having apologized for his anti-Jewish order in 1868, he became highly sensitive, even hypersensitive, to Jewish concerns. He came to appreciate the diversity of Jews, displaying particular appreciation for those who pulled themselves up, as he himself had done, from poverty to respectability. He appointed more Jews to public office than any of his predecessors. He sought to bring Jews (as well as Blacks) into the mainstream of American political life. He acted to promote human rights for Jews around the world.

Who is buried in Grant's Tomb?" the Jewish comedian Groucho Marx used to ask down-and-out contestants on his popular 1950s quiz show, *You Bet Your Life*. The question, while always good for a laugh (in fact, Ulysses and Julia Grant were "entombed" and not "buried" there at all), concealed a deep truth. By the 1950s, Ulysses S. Grant had become a mystery and a caricature to many of his countrymen. His tomb was neglected, the memory of his achievements obscured.

Careful reexamination of the record by historians, in recent years, has revised the image of the man "buried" in Grant's Tomb. New biographies set forth many of his political achievements, especially in the area of race. A 2008 poll of top international and political commentators lifted him, for the first time ever, into the second quartile of American presidents, ranking him as number 18.[36]

Grant's record with respect to Jews now likewise requires revision. During his administration, Jews moved from outsider to insider status in the United States, and from weakness to strength. Having abruptly expelled Jews in 1862, Grant as president significantly empowered them. He insisted, over the objections of those who propounded narrower visions of America, that the country could embrace people of different races, religions, and creeds. He endeavored, as president, to further human rights at home and abroad.

Reconstruction is an ongoing and never-ending process in America. Over time, albeit in fits and starts, with forward steps and backward ones, freedom and human rights have advanced. Innumerable mistakes have been made along the way, from which Jews, African Americans, and other minority groups have suffered grievously. Fortunately, many of these mistakes have, over the course of time, been corrected.

So it was with General Orders No. 11. Its unexpected aftermath—the transformation of Ulysses S. Grant from enemy to friend, from Haman to Mordecai, from a general who expelled "Jews as a class" to a president who embraced Jews as individuals—reminds us that even great figures in history can learn from their mistakes.

In America, hatred can be overcome.

CHRONOLOGY

1492   Jews of Spain are expelled by King Ferdinand and Queen Isabella. Any who remain are required to convert to Christianity and subject to the Inquisition, which seeks out and executes crypto-Jews.

Christopher Columbus sets out on a voyage funded by King Ferdinand and Queen Isabella, seeking a shorter route to India. He alights upon North America instead.

1630   The Netherlands capture Pernambuco, Brazil, from the Portuguese and invites Jewish settlement. A significant Jewish community develops in Recife.

1654   Portugal recaptures Brazil and expels Jews and Protestants. While most Jews return to the Netherlands, a boatload of twenty-three Jews, mostly of Iberian descent, sails into New Amsterdam.

1655   Jews win the right to settle in New Amsterdam and establish a Jewish community.

1678   Jewish cemetery set up in Newport, Rhode Island.

1730   New York Jews build North America's first synagogue, Shearith Israel, on Mill Street.

1763   Newport Jews dedicate Yeshuat Israel Synagogue. Later known as the Touro Synagogue, it is the only surviving colonial synagogue structure.

1776   The Continental Congress adopts the Declaration of Independence. The War of Independence follows.

Chronology

1788   Ratification of the United States Constitution permits Jews to hold federal office.

1790   George Washington visits Newport and, in response to an address from its Jews, describes religious liberty as an inherent natural right. He declares that the government of the United States offers "to bigotry no sanction, to persecution no assistance."

December 15, 1791   The Bill of Rights, which comprises the first ten amendments to the Constitution, is ratified. The First Amendment forbids Congress from making any laws "respecting an establishment of religion or prohibiting the free exercise thereof."

April 27, 1822   Hiram Ulysses Grant is born to Jesse Root Grant and Hannah Simpson Grant in Point Pleasant, Clermont County, Ohio.

May 29, 1839   Grant enters the U.S. Military Academy at West Point. He is registered incorrectly as Ulysses Simpson Grant and uses that name going forward.

1840   Prominent Syrian Jews are falsely accused of the ritual murder of an Italian monk in Damascus; American Jews lobby for the U.S. government to intercede on their behalf.

September 30, 1843   Having graduated from West Point in the middle of his class (twenty-first in a class of thirty-nine), Grant reports for duty at Jefferson Barracks in Missouri.

1843   Establishment of the Jewish fraternal organization B'nai B'rith, which aims to preserve Jewish life on the basis of the covenantal ties linking Jews to one another.

April 25, 1846   Mexico declares war on the United States after Zachary Taylor's army, in which Grant is serving, crosses disputed territory.

May 30, 1848   The Treaty of Guadalupe Hidalgo marks the end of the Mexican War.

August 22, 1848   Grant marries Julia Dent in St. Louis, Missouri.

November 1848   Grant is assigned to a barracks in Sackets Harbor, New York. In nearby Watertown, New York, he meets and befriends Jesse and Henry Seligman at their dry goods store.

1853   Isaac Leeser, America's foremost traditional Jewish religious leader and the editor of *The Occident*, completes his translation of the Bible into English. It is the first complete Anglo-Jewish translation of the Bible.

1854   Isaac Mayer Wise, who immigrated to the United States in 1846, assumes a rabbinical pulpit in Cincinnati, promising to shape an American form of Judaism. He begins to publish the *Israelite* (later *American Israelite*) newspaper.

April 11, 1854   Grant resigns from the army.

Summer 1854   Grant settles on the Dent family farm in Missouri.

1858   Cesar Kaskel emigrates from Prussia to America, settling in Paducah, Kentucky.

Chronology

1858–59   American Jews join Jews worldwide in campaigning
           for the release of Edgardo Mortara, a Jewish boy
           who had been secretly baptized by a Catholic maid
           and then seized by the Catholic Church.

1859   Board of Delegates of American Israelites founded
        "to keep a watchful eye on all occurrences at home
        and abroad" and to collect statistics. It represents
        less than a fifth of America's synagogues.

February 1, 1860   Rabbi Morris J. Raphall becomes the first Jewish
                    clergyman to offer a prayer at the opening of a
                    session of Congress.

Spring 1860   Grant moves to Galena, Illinois, where he works in
               his father's dry goods store.

December 20, 1860   South Carolina secedes from the United States
                     following the election of Abraham Lincoln; ten
                     additional Southern states secede over the next six
                     months.

March 4, 1861   Abraham Lincoln is inaugurated president of the
                 United States.

April 12, 1861   Southern forces open fire on the Union fortifications
                  at Fort Sumter, igniting what will become the Civil
                  War.

May 4, 1861   Grant becomes commanding officer at Camp Yates,
               Springfield, Illinois.

July 31, 1861   Ulysses S. Grant nominated by Abraham Lincoln
                 as brigadier general. The Senate confirms the
                 appointment on August 5.

September 6, 1861 Grant and the Union army occupy Paducah, Kentucky.

September 17, 1861 Judah P. Benjamin named acting secretary of war of the Confederate States of America; he was subsequently confirmed in that position and in 1862 was named secretary of state.

February 1862 Grant's forces capture Fort Henry and Fort Donelson in Tennessee, opening the Tennessee and Cumberland rivers to the Union army; Grant promoted to major general.

June 6, 1862 Union forces capture Memphis, Tennessee. Grant establishes his military headquarters there on June 23.

July 17, 1862 Military chaplaincy law amended. Instead of restricting chaplains to ministers of "some Christian denomination," the chaplaincy is now opened up to ministers of "some religious denomination," including rabbis.

July 26, 1862 Grant orders the commander of the District of Mississippi to examine the baggage of all south-bound speculators, especially Jews.

October 25, 1862 Grant assumes command over the Department of the Tennessee, extending from Cairo, Illinois, to northern Mississippi, bounded by the Tennessee and Mississippi rivers.

November 9–10, 1862 As he prepares to move south, Grant restricts permits for Jews to enter the Department of the Tennessee.

November 29, 1862	Grant establishes headquarters at Holly Springs, Mississippi.
December 8, 1862	Colonel John Van Deusen Du Bois orders "All Cotton-Speculators [and] Jews" to leave Holly Springs, Mississippi. Grant overturns the order.
December 17, 1862	Grant issues General Orders No. 11, expelling all Jews from the territory under his command.
December 20, 1862	Confederate general Earl Van Dorn attacks Grant's forces at Holly Springs, cutting rail and telegraph lines and destroying supplies.
December 28, 1862	Pursuant to Grant's General Orders No. 11, all Jews are expelled from Paducah, Kentucky. Cesar Kaskel and others respond by sending an urgent telegram to President Lincoln.
December 30, 1862	The story of the expulsion of the Jews appears in several newspapers.
December 31, 1862	General in Chief Henry Halleck reads Kaskel's telegram.
January 1, 1863	Abraham Lincoln issues the Emancipation Proclamation, freeing all Confederate-held slaves.
January 3, 1863	Kaskel arrives in Washington, D.C. Accompanied by ousted Cincinnati congressman John Addison Gurley, he successfully appeals to Lincoln to countermand Grant's order.
January 4, 1863	On Lincoln's instruction, Halleck orders Grant to revoke the order.

January 5, 1863   Senator Lazarus Powell of Kentucky proposes a resolution in the Senate denouncing General Orders No. 11.

January 6, 1863   On Halleck's instruction, Grant revokes General Orders No. 11.

January 7, 1863   Representative George H. Pendleton of Ohio proposes a resolution in the House of Representatives denouncing General Orders No. 11.

A delegation of Jewish leaders including Rabbi Isaac Mayer Wise meets with President Lincoln to thank him for revoking the order. Lincoln reiterates that he "knows of no distinction between Jew and Gentile" and declares that he does "not like to hear a class or nationality condemned on account of a few sinners."

January 9, 1863   U.S. Senate tables a resolution rebuking Grant for General Orders No. 11.

July 4, 1863   Vicksburg, Mississippi, surrenders to Grant's forces, ending a seven-week siege. The victory gives the Union control over the entire Mississippi River and splits the Confederacy in two.

February 11, 1864   A delegation from the National Reform Association approaches Lincoln seeking his support for a constitutional amendment that would make America an explicitly Christian country.

March 9, 1864   Grant, a national hero, is promoted to the rank of lieutenant general, previously held by George Washington. He is assigned to command the armies of the United States.

Chronology

November 8, 1864   Abraham Lincoln elected to a second term as president.

April 9, 1865   Robert E. Lee surrenders to Grant at Appomattox Court House, Virginia.

April 14, 1865   Abraham Lincoln is shot by John Wilkes Booth and dies the next day.

1866   Grant moves to Washington, D.C., and is appointed general of the armies of the United States.

May 21, 1868   Grant wins the Republican nomination for the presidency.

May 26, 1868   Impeachment trial of President Andrew Johnson ends; he is acquitted by one vote.

May 29, 1868   Grant accepts the nomination for president of the United States.

July 9, 1868   Ratification of the Fourteenth Amendment, which guarantees citizenship to anyone born on U.S. soil.

July 1868   Reports circulate that large numbers of Jews are planning to vote against Grant on account of General Orders No. 11.

September 14, 1868   In a private letter to former Illinois congressman Isaac Newton Morris, Grant disavows General Orders No. 11. Morris shares the letter with B'nai B'rith leader Adolph Moses.

October 13, 1868   Adolph Moses declares his support for Grant in a letter published in the *New York Times*.

November 3, 1868	Grant is elected president of the United States.
November 27–30, 1868	Newspapers publish and celebrate Grant's letter declaring that he did not sustain General Orders No. 11, was free of prejudice, and wanted "each individual to be judged by his own merit."
March 4, 1869	Grant is inaugurated as the eighteenth president of the United States.
April 17, 1869	Grant nominates Simon Wolf to the position of recorder of deeds for the District of Columbia; in this capacity he also advises Grant on Jewish matters.
April 20, 1869	Rabbi Haim Zvi Sneersohn visits Grant in the White House, blesses him, and calls for the replacement of America's consul to Jerusalem, Victor Beauboucher, as well as for support of the Jews in the Holy Land.
1869	Some two thousand Jews are expelled from the Bessarabian frontier, in accordance with an 1825 Russian law that forbids Jews from living near Russia's borders. American Jews ask Grant to intercede on behalf of their coreligionists and he agrees to do so. The expulsion order is revoked.
September 24, 1869	"Black Friday" spells the end of an audacious effort by Jay Gould and James Fisk to corner the market in gold. Since Grant hinted to his friends the Seligmans that they should disassociate themselves from Gould, they emerge unscathed.

January 10, 1870 — Grant appoints Wolf's friend Edward S. Salomon governor of the Washington Territory.

February 3, 1870 — Ratification of the Fifteenth Amendment, which guarantees voting rights to citizens of all races.

June 1870 — Reports of massacres of Jews in Romania reach the American public; American Jews campaign for a U.S. consul to Romania who can help ease the situation.

June 29, 1870 — Grant's nomination of Benjamin F. Peixotto as consul to Romania approved by the Senate.

January 12, 1871 — Grant's appointment of Dr. Herman Bendell, a Jew, as superintendent of Indian affairs for the Arizona Territory is approved by the Senate, notwithstanding the government's stated policy of "Christianization" for Native Americans.

January 1872 — Salomon tenders his resignation after having been caught embezzling funds.

November 4, 1872 — Grant wins reelection, carrying thirty-one of thirty-seven states.

July 8, 1873 — Founding conference, in Cincinnati, of the Union of American Hebrew Congregations, an umbrella organization of synagogues dedicated to preserving Judaism and encouraging Jewish education (today known as the Union for Reform Judaism).

September 30, 1875 — Grant, in an address to the Army of the Tennessee reunion in Des Moines, champions church-state separation and nonsectarian public education.

October 3, 1875	Opening of Hebrew Union College in Cincinnati, the first successful rabbinical seminary in America.
June 9, 1876	Grant attends dedication of Adas Israel, an Orthodox synagogue in Washington, D.C., becoming the first American president to attend a synagogue dedication.
July 12, 1876	Grant meets his former antagonist Rabbi Isaac Mayer Wise when welcoming leaders of the Union of American Hebrew Congregations at the White House.
March 5, 1877	Rutherford B. Hayes inaugurated following a disputed election; Grant leaves the White House.
May 17, 1877	Grant, with his wife and son, embarks on a world tour.
June 13, 1877	Wealthy Jewish banker Joseph Seligman, a friend of Grant's, is excluded from the Grand Union Hotel in Saratoga, New York, on account of his religion, sparking a national outcry.
February 11–17, 1878	Grant and party tour the Holy Land; he is the first American president ever to visit there.
December 16, 1879	Grant completes his world tour in Philadelphia; he settles in New York and becomes an investment banker.
March 13, 1881	Assassination of Tsar Alexander II sparks an orgy of anti-Jewish violence in Russia and stimulates Jewish immigration to the United States.

May 17, 1881   President Garfield appoints Frederick Douglass to the position of recorder of deeds.

February 1, 1882   Public meeting in support of Russia's persecuted Jews, endorsed by Grant.

April 13, 1885   Grant, suffering from cancer, receives the well wishes of "the Rabbis of New York and adjacent States."

July 23, 1885   Grant is pronounced dead at 8:08 a.m. Jews join in national mourning.

August 8, 1885   Grant is entombed in New York; Rabbi Edward Benjamin Morris Browne is among the pallbearers. Since it is the Jewish Sabbath, he walks the seven-and-a-half-mile route from City Hall to the place of entombment.

January 2, 1887   Jewish Theological Seminary opens in New York to serve "Jews of America faithful to Mosaic law and ancestral tradition." Over time it becomes the training ground for Conservative rabbis.

March 8, 1897   Rabbi Isaac Elchanan Theological Seminary incorporated in New York, the first advanced Talmudic academy in the United States. Now part of Yeshiva University, it trains Orthodox rabbis.

April 27, 1897   Grant's Tomb is opened in New York's Riverside Park. Jews participate in the "Grant parade" that marks the occasion, and Rabbi Joseph Silverman in advance of the event delivers a stirring sermon on "Let Us Have Peace."

1906   President Theodore Roosevelt appoints Oscar S. Straus to the position of secretary of commerce and labor, making him the first Jew to hold a cabinet position.

1912 Henrietta Szold founds Hadassah, the Women's Zionist Organization of America.

1916 Louis Brandeis, the "people's lawyer" and, since 1914, the leader of the Zionist movement, becomes America's first Jewish Supreme Court justice.

1924 Johnson-Reed Act passes. It goes into effect the next year, significantly limiting immigration to the United States and privileging immigrants from Northern and Western Europe. Average Jewish immigration to the United States plummets from almost 100,000 per year to just over 8,000.

1925 Jewish population in America reaches approximately 4 million out of 115 million, or 3.5 percent of the U.S. population.

NOTES

Abbreviations and Short Titles

AJA   American Jewish Archives, Cincinnati, Ohio

AJA   *American Jewish Archives* (Journal)

AJHS   American Jewish Historical Society, New York

EJ   *Encyclopaedia Judaica* (1972, 2007)

OR   *The War of the Rebellion: A Compilation of the Official Records of the Union and Confederate Armies.* Washington, D.C.: Government Printing Office, 1880–1901; online at http://digital.library.cornell.edu/m/moawar/waro.html

PAJHS   *Publications of the American Jewish Historical Society*

PUSG   *The Papers of Ulysses S. Grant*, ed. John Y. Simon, 31 vols. Carbondale: Southern Illinois University Press, 1967–2009; online at http://digital.library.msstate.edu/collections/index.php?CISOROOT=/usgrant

Korn, *American Jewry and the Civil War.* Bertram Wallace Korn, *American Jewry and the Civil War.* New York: Atheneum, 1970.

McFeely, *Grant.* William S. McFeely, *Grant: A Biography.* New York: W. W. Norton, 1981.

Panitz, *Simon Wolf.* Esther L. Panitz, *Simon Wolf: Private Conscience and Public Image.* Rutherford, N.J.: Fairleigh Dickinson University Press, 1987.

Smith, *Grant.* Jean Edward Smith, *Grant.* New York: Simon & Schuster, 2001.

Wolf, *Presidents I Have Known.* Simon Wolf, *The Presidents I Have Known from 1860–1918.* Washington, D.C.: Press of Byron S. Adams, 1918.

Introduction

1. *EJ* (2nd ed.), 8:35. The identical quote appeared in the first edition.

2. See now the family's unpublished memoir, "General Orders No. 11: The Mack Brothers—Real Trouble Makers" in AJA. It reveals that Buddy Mack "only begrudgingly" acknowledged Grant's episode with his great-grandfather.

3. David Quigley, *Second Founding: New York City, Reconstruction and the Making of American Democracy* (New York: Hill and Wang, 2004).

4. Constitution of the National Reform Association, http://candst.tripod.com/nra.htm.

5. Eric Foner, *Reconstruction: America's Unfinished Revolution, 1863–1877* (New York: Harper Perennial, 2002).

6. *American Israelite* (May 20, 1881), 364.

7. *American Hebrew* (December 10, 1897), 163.

8. *American Israelite* (July 31, 1885).

9. *New York Times* (March 13, 2010).

10. *New York Times* (March 22, 2010).

1. General Orders No. 11

1. For biographical information on Kaskel, see *Hamagid* 7 (1863): 84; Isaac Markens, "Lincoln and the Jews," *PAJHS* 17 (1909): 117–19; and Kaskel's own statement to the press, December 30, 1862, a copy of which is in SC-4218, AJA. Jacob Kaskel is mentioned in J. Cohn, *Geschichte der jüdischen Gemeinde Rawitsch* (Berlin: L. Lam, 1915), 69. On Paducah, see Isaac W. Bernheim, *History of the Settlement of Jews in Paducah and the Lower Ohio Valley* (Paducah, Ky.: Temple Israel, 1912); Amy Hill Shevitz, *Jewish Communities on the Ohio River: A History* (Louisville: University Press of Kentucky, 2007), 98–101; John E. L. Robertson, "Paducah: Origins to Second Class," *Register of the Kentucky Historical Society* 66 (1968): 108–36; John E. L. Robertson, *Paducah: Frontier to the Atomic Age* (Charleston, S.C.: Arcadia Books, 2002).

2. Ulysses S. Grant, *Memoirs and Selected Letters: Personal Memoirs of U. S. Grant, Selected Letters, 1839–1865* (New York: Library of America, 1990), 175.

3. Markens, "Lincoln and the Jews," 118; *Hamagid* 7 (1863): 84; Joseph S. Kaskel to Bertram W. Korn (October 7, 1950), Bertram W. Korn Papers, box 6, file 5, AJA.

4. Stephen V. Ash, "Civil War Exodus: The Jews and Grant's General Orders No. 11," *The Historian* 44 (August 1982): 505–23, esp. 514–17; S. L. Phelps to A. H. Foote (December 30, 1861) in *Official Records of the Union and Confederate Navies in the War of the Rebellion* (Washington: Government Printing Office, 1908), series I, vol. 22, p. 479.

5. This and subsequent quotes are from Kaskel's statement to the press (December 30, 1862), SC-4218, AJA.

6. Korn, *American Jewry and the Civil War*, 123; Robertson, *Paducah: Frontier to the Atomic Age*, 44.

7. Korn, *American Jewry and the Civil War*, 122.

8. Sylvanus Cadwallader, *Three Years with Grant*, ed. Benjamin P. Thomas (New York: Alfred A. Knopf, 1955), 32–40, quote on 36; N. P. Chipman to Samuel R. Curtis (December 24, 1862) in *OR*, series I, vol. 17 (part 2), 471; Grant to Commanding

Officer Expedition Down Mississippi (December 23, 1862), in *OR*, series I, vol. 17 (part 2), 463: "These raids have cut off communication, so that I have had nothing from the north for over a week." For background on these raids, see James M. McPherson, *Battle Cry of Freedom: The Civil War Era* (New York: Oxford University Press, 1988), 578; David J. Eicher, *The Longest Night: A Military History of the Civil War* (New York: Touchstone, 2001), 388–90.

9. Yosef Hayim Yerushalmi, *"Servants of Kings and Not Servants of Servants": Some Aspects of the Political History of the Jews*, The Tenenbaum Family Lecture Series in Judaic Studies (Atlanta: Emory University, 2005), 7.

10. *OR*, series I, vol. 17 (part 2), 506. The "official record" slightly diverges in wording and spelling from the original, reprinted in *PUSG* 7, p. 54. Robertson, *Paducah: Frontier to the Atomic Age*, 44, identifies Wolff as "David," but Bernheim, *History of the Settlement of Jews in Paducah*, quoting the 1859 Paducah City Directory, provides the names of all three brothers, none of whom was known as David. In writing to Lincoln they identified themselves as "D. Wolff & Bros."

11. Isaac Mayer Wise claimed that Lincoln "informed General Halleck instantly" upon receipt of Kaskel's telegram, but no external evidence supports this. See *Israelite* (January 16, 1863), 218.

12. *Memphis Daily Bulletin* (January 6, 1863), as cited in Korn, *American Jewry and the Civil War*, 272n16.

13. *PUSG* 7, p. 55. Grant's "report" on January 15, 1863, consisted simply of copies "of General Orders from this Department."

14. A copy of Kaskel's statement to the press (December 30, 1862) is found in SC-4218, AJA, photocopied from an unidentified clipping. It appeared in the *Cincinnati Daily Enquirer* (January 2, 1863), in the *Memphis Daily Bulletin* (January 6, 1863), and in the New York *Jewish Record* (January 9, 1863). Korn, *American Jewry and the Civil War*, 124, identifies the steamer as the *"Charley Bowens"* and Kaskel calls it the *"Chaley Bowe,"* but it was in all likelihood Captain Henry T. Dexter's *Charley Bowen*; see Myron J. Smith Jr., *The Timberclads in the Civil War* (Jefferson, N.C.: McFarland, 2008), 38, 65, 90.

15. Markens, "Lincoln and the Jews," 118, has him arriving by steamer in Cairo, Illinois, on his way to Washington. The *Israelite* never mentions that Kaskel was in Cincinnati or that Isaac Mayer Wise met him, but it does mention the letters he collected from Lilienthal and Wolf. Korn, *American Jewry and the Civil War*, 124, concludes from this that Kaskel paused in Cincinnati "only momentarily," which is plausible but not certain.

16. *Israelite* (June 14, 1861), 396; Sefton D. Temkin, "Isaac Mayer Wise and the Civil War," *AJA* 15 (1963): 120–42; Jonathan D. Sarna, *American Judaism: A History* (New Haven, Conn.: Yale University Press, 2004), 96–98.

17. *Israelite* (January 2, 1863), 202.

18. Isaac M. Wise to Edward [*sic*] Stanton (December 30, 1862), Isaac Mayer Wise Digital Archive, http://www.americanjewisharchives.org/wise/view.php?id=2630 (accessed October 15, 2009).

19. Isaac M. Wise to Edward [*sic*] M. Stanton (January 4, 1863), Isaac Mayer Wise Digital Archive, http://www.americanjewisharchives.org/wise/view.php?id=2631 (accessed October 15, 2009).

20. This undated clipping [January 6, 1863?], and a similar one attributed to the Washington correspondent of the *New York Tribune*, is found in Jacob R. Marcus's collection of "Civil War Documents," now in AJA.

21. Robert Shosteck, "The Jewish Community of Washington, D.C., During the Civil War," *American Jewish Historical Quarterly* 56 (1966–67): 334–35; Adolphus Solomons to Henry S. Hart (January 6, 1863), Board of Delegates of American Israelites Papers, AJHS. Myer Isaacs, "The Board of Delegates of American Israelites: Final Report," *PAJHS* 29 (1925): 106, declares that Adolphus Solomons "represented to the President and the Secretary of War the illegal, unjust and tyrannical character" of Grant's order, and implies that this affected the course of events. Neither the board's own papers at AJHS nor any other source warrants such a conclusion.

22. United Order of Bne Brith Missouri Loge [*sic*] to His Excellency Abr. Lincoln (January 5, 1863), copy in Philip Lax Archive/Archives of B'nai B'rith, Washington, D.C., and in S-C 4218, *AJA*; Korn, *American Jewry and the Civil War*, 126.

23. Sarna, *American Judaism*, 112, 375; Ash, "Civil War Exodus," 513.

24. *Israelite* (January 2, 1863), 202; *Jewish Record* (N.Y.) (January 13, 1863), online at http://www.jewish-history.com/civilwar/go11.htm (accessed October 16, 2009).

25. Spiegel was the highest-ranking Jewish officer under Grant's command; see John Y. Simon, "That Obnoxious Order," *Civil War Times Illustrated* 23, no. 6 (1984): 14, and *A Jewish Colonel in the Civil War: Marcus M. Spiegel of the Ohio Volunteers*, ed. Jean Powers Soman and Frank K. Byrne (Lincoln: University of Nebraska Press, 1995); on Trounstine see chapter 2, and Cadwallader, *Three Years with Grant*, 40.

26. Telegrams concerning General Orders No. 11 and Jewish sutlers are listed in *PUSG* 7, p. 53. On sutlers, see "sutler," *Oxford English Dictionary*, online at http://dictionary.oed.com.resources.library.brandeis.edu/cgi/entry/50243710, and David Michael Delo, *Peddlers and Post Traders: The Army Sutler on the Frontier* (Salt Lake City: University of Utah Press, 1992). Friedrich von Hayek noted other examples of less respected trades opened up to alien races; see Jerry Z. Muller, *Capitalism and the Jews* (Princeton, N.J.: Princeton University Press, 2009), 67.

27. *Israelite* (January 23, 1863), 229; on Sullivan, see Ezra J. Warner, *Generals in Blue: Lives of the Union Commanders* (Baton Rouge: Louisiana State University Press, 1964), 487–88.

28. Korn, *American Jewry and the Civil War*, 125; Markens, "Lincoln and the Jews," 118.

29. *Israelite* (January 16, 1863), 218; *PUSG* 7, pp. 53–54; a follow-up circular letter went out the next day (January 7) with essentially the same text; see *OR*, series I, vol. 17 (part 2), 544.

30. Markens, "Lincoln and the Jews," 119.

31. Kelton to Grant (January 5, 1863) in *PUSG* 7, p. 54; *OR*, series I, vol. 24 (part 1), 9.

32. *Philadelphia Inquirer* (January 6, 1863), 2; [Baltimore] *Sun* (January 6, 1863); undated clippings in Jacob R. Marcus's collection of "Civil War Documents," now in AJA; Adolphus Solomons to Henry S. Hart (January 6, 1863), Board of Delegates of American Israelites Papers, AJHS; *Israelite* (January 16, 1863), 218.

33. *Israelite* (January 16, 1863), 218; the article was reprinted as far away as San Francisco: *San Francisco Daily Evening Bulletin* (February 10, 1863).

2. "Jews as a Class"

1. *Biographical Sketch of the Honorable Lazarus W. Powell* (Frankfurt, Ky.: S.I.M Major Public Printer, 1868), quotes are from 61, 63, 73; E. Merton Coulter, "Powell, Lazarus Whitehead," *Dictionary of American Biography*, vol. 15 (New York: Scribner's 1935), 148–49; Mark E. Neely, *The Fate of Liberty: Abraham Lincoln and Civil Liberties* (New York: Oxford University Press, 1991).

2. *Journal of the Senate*, 37th Congress, 3rd Session (January 5, 1863), 78; *Congressional Globe*, Senate, 37th Congress, 3rd Session (January 9, 1863), 245.

3. *Congressional Globe*, 37th Congress, 3rd Session (January 7, 1863), part 1, p. 222; *Journal of the House of Representatives*, 37th Congress 3rd session (January 7, 1863), 151; E. B. Washburne to Abraham Lincoln (January 6, 1863), Robert Todd Lincoln Collection, reprinted in Korn, *American Jewry and the Civil War*, 273 (copy of the original in Jacob Rader Marcus Papers, Civil War box 1, AJA); Ari Hoogenboom, "Pendleton, George Hunt," *American National Biography Online* (accessed October 25, 2009). For the importance of Washburne's support to Grant, see Julia Dent Grant, *The Personal Memoirs of Julia Dent Grant*, ed. John Y. Simon (New York: Putnam, 1975), 107.

4. *Congressional Globe*, 37th Congress, 3rd Session (January 9, 1863), 245–46; *Biographical Sketch of the Honorable Lazarus W. Powell*, 73–76.

5. *Congressional Globe*, 37th Congress, 3rd Session (January 9, 1863), 245–46.

6. *Cincinnati Commercial* (January 6, 1863); *Cincinnati Enquirer* (January 3, 1863); Korn, *American Jewry and the Civil War*, 128–30; *New York Times* (January 18, 1863), 4.

7. "On Persecution," *The Occident* 20 (February–March 1863), online at http://www.jewish-history.com/civilwar/on_persecution.html#Related_Pages (accessed October 27, 2009). Leeser's understanding of "exile" follows the Talmudic teaching in TB Brachot 34b, Sanhedrin 99a.

8. Ibid.; Eli Evans, *Judah P. Benjamin: The Jewish Confederate* (New York: Free Press, 1989), esp. 97; Korn, *American Jewry and the Civil War*, xx, 158–59; Neely, *The Fate of Liberty*, 107–9.

9. *Harper's Weekly* (August 1, 1863), as quoted in Korn, *American Jewry and the Civil War*, xxi; Gary L. Bunker and John Appel, " 'Shoddy,' Anti-Semitism and the Civil War," *American Jewish History* 82 (1994): 43–71; Frederic Cople Jaher, *A Scapegoat in the New Wilderness: The Origins and Rise of Anti-Semitism in America* (Cambridge, Mass.: Harvard University Press, 1994), 190–203, 223–26; Ellis Rivkin, "A Decisive Pattern in American Jewish History," in *Essays in American Jewish History* (Cincinnati: AJA, 1958), 38.

10. Philip Trounstine to Major C. S. Hayes (March 3, 1863) online at http://www.jewish-history.com/civilwar/trnstine.htm. Sylvanus Cadwallader, *Three Years with Grant*, ed. Benjamin P. Thomas (New York: Alfred A. Knopf, 1955), 40, reports that Trounstine "was the only cavalry officer in the service that was of Hebraic extraction. He enlisted early and served creditably to the end."

11. *OR*, series I, vol. 17 (part 2), 172; series III, vol. 2, 350; series I, vol. 20 (part 2), 114; series I, vol. 15, 583. James M. McPherson, *Battle Cry of Freedom: The Civil War Era* (New York: Oxford University Press, 1988), 624, discusses Butler and the cotton trade. In a revealing correspondence with Myer Isaacs of the Board of Delegates, Butler showed how little he knew about Jews, identifying as "Jews" several Confederates who were not Jewish at all. "My experience with men of the Jewish faith or nation," he confessed, "has been an unfortunate one." The correspondence is reprinted in *PAJHS* 29 (1925): 119–30.

12. Morris U. Schappes, *A Documentary History of the Jews in the United States, 1654–1875* (New York: Citadel Press, 1950), 80; A. M. Waddell as quoted in Leonard Rogoff, *Down Home: Jewish Life in North Carolina* (Chapel Hill: University of North Carolina Press, 2010), 96. Waddell, a white supremacist, later played a central role in the 1898 Wilmington insurrection and riot. For "as a class" references, see *OR*, series I, vol. 47 (part 3), 461; *OR*, series I, vol. 22 (part 1), 814; *OR*, series III, vol. 3, 516; *Official Records of the Union and Confederate Navies in the War of the Rebellion*, series I, vol. 25, 474.

13. *OR*, series I, vol. 17 (part 2), 240; *OR*, series I, vol. 22 (part 2), 473; McPherson, *Battle Cry of Freedom*, 785–86; Neely, *The Fate of Freedom*, 46–49; Charles R. Mink, "General Orders, No. 11: The Forced Evacuation of Civilians During the Civil War," *Military Affairs* 34 (December 1980): 132–37.

14. Stephen V. Ash, "Civil War Exodus: The Jews and Grant's General Orders No. 11," *The Historian* 44 (August 1982): 511; Korn, *American Jewry and the Civil War*, 279n70.

15. H. H. Ben Sasson, "Expulsions," *EJ* (2nd ed., 2007), 6:624–26; Yosef Hayim Yerushalmi, "Exile and Expulsion in Jewish History," in Benjamin R. Gampel, *Crisis and Creativity in the Sephardic World, 1391–1648* (New York: Columbia University

Press, 1997), 3–22. As late as 1938, according to one poll, one-fifth of all Americans wanted to "drive Jews out of the United States." Charles Stember, *Jews in the Mind of America* (New York: Basic Books, 1966), 121–23.

16. *Israelite* 9 (February 20, 1863), 258; on the Associated Press, see Menahem Blondheim, *News over the Wires: The Telegraph and the Flow of Public Information in America, 1844–1897* (Cambridge, Mass.: Harvard, 1994), quote from p. 130.

17. I have found but two references to this theme: a polemical footnote in Schappes, *A Documentary History*, 704n16; and a single paragraph in Korn, *American Jewry and the Civil War*, 132.

18. Louis Ruchames, "The Abolitionists and the Jews: Some Further Thoughts," in *A Bicentennial Festschrift for Jacob Rader Marcus*, ed. Bertram W. Korn (New York: Ktav, 1976), 508, 511; *Israelite* 9 (January 16, 1863), 218; reprinted in Schappes, *A Documentary History*, 475.

19. Eric Goldstein, *The Price of Whiteness: Jews, Race, and American Identity* (Princeton, N.J.: Princeton University Press, 2006) masterfully explores this theme.

20. [New York] *Jewish Record* (January 23, 1863); Korn, *American Jewry and the Civil War*, 132.

21. *The Occident* 20 (Feb.–March 1863): 498–99; see also his prejudiced comments on 493, 497. Also available online at http://www.jewish-history.com/civilwar/on_persecution.html.

22. John V. D. Du Bois, "General Orders No. 2," as quoted in *PUSG* 7, p. 9n1; for related complaints see p. 51n.

23. David G. Surdam, "Traders or Traitors: Northern Cotton Trading During the Civil War," *Business and Economic History* 28 (Winter 1999): 301–12, esp. 302; Stanley Lebergott, "Through the Blockade: The Profitability and Extent of Cotton Smuggling, 1861–1865," *Journal of Economic History* 41 (December 1981): 867–88.

24. Grant to Christopher P. Wolcott (December 17, 1862) in *PUSG* 7, pp. 56–57; *OR*, series I, vol. 17 (part 2), 141; *OR*, series I, vol. 25 (part 2), 80; McPherson, *Battle Cry of Freedom*, 600–625; Joseph H. Parks, "A Confederate Trade Center Under Federal Occupation: Memphis, 1862 to 1865," *Journal of Southern History* 7 (August 1941): 289–314.

25. Salo Baron, *The Russian Jew Under Tsars and Soviets* (New York: Schocken Books, 1987), 33, 85–86.

26. This communication, likely from 1863, is reprinted in Moritz Ellinger, *History of Washington Lodge No. 19 Independent Order B'nai B'rith* (New York: n.p., 1904), 12.

27. Heyman Herzberg, "Civil War Adventures of a Georgia Merchant," in Jacob R. Marcus, *Memoirs of American Jews* (Philadelphia: Jewish Publication Society, 1956), 3:116–32 (typescript of original in the AJA).

28. Marcus, *Memoirs of American Jews*, 2:138–39. Emanuel and Mayer Lehman, founders of the eponymous banking firm, were likewise blockade-runners: "Mayer maneuvered whatever cotton he could through the blockade, and Emanuel sold it to an

eager market in New York"; see Peter Chapman, *The Last of the Imperious Rich: Lehman Brothers, 1844–2008* (New York: Portfolio/Penguin, 2010), 28–29.

29. A. E. Frankland, "Kronikals of the Times—Memphis, 1862," *AJA* 9 (October 1957): 83–125; see also Judy G. Ringel, *Children of Israel: The Story of Temple Israel, Memphis, Tennessee: 1854–2004* (Memphis: Temple Israel Books, 2004), 11–13.

30. Chicago *Times* as quoted in Parks, "A Confederate Trade Center," 293; Albert Richardson, *A Personal History of Ulysses S. Grant* (Hartford, Conn.: American Publishing Company, 1868), 276; Charles A. Dana to Edwin M. Stanton (January 21, 1863) in *OR*, series I, vol. 52 (part 1), 331; S. A. Hurlbut to John A. Rawlins (March 7, 1863) in *OR*, series I, vol. 24 (part 3), 92. On Dana as a cotton speculator, see McFeely, *Grant*, 123.

31. See *OR*, series I, vol. 11 (part 3), 336, for intelligence provided by "an intelligent Jew boy, fourteen years of age, who is right from Richmond"; and *OR*, series I, vol. 30 (part 4), 4–8, for the remarkable report by twenty-year-old Jewish immigrant Louis Trager, "a freelance intelligence operative, purveying information to the Union Army, which he picked up on business trips and visits to the Confederacy"; cf. Milton M. Grossman, *Hoopskirts and Huppas: A Chronicle of the Early Years of the Garfunkel-Trager Family in America* (New York: AJHS, 1999), 17.

32. Ulysses S. Grant, *Memoirs and Selected Letters: Personal Memoirs of U. S. Grant, Selected Letters, 1839–1865* (New York: Library of America, 1990), 266–67; Grant to Salmon P. Chase (July 31, 1862), reprinted in ibid., 1010–11.

33. *PUSG* 6, p. 238; 7, p. 52n; 6, p. 283 (and note); 6, pp. 393–94.

34. *PUSG* 7, pp. 8–9. In 1868, Du Bois claimed that his "order was revoked by Gen Grant and I was relieved from command on account of it." Du Bois to Editor of the *Morning Chronicle*, Washington, D.C. (September 29, 1868), typescript in Civil War Documents, Jacob R. Marcus Papers, AJA.

35. Lee M. Friedman, "Something Additional on General Grant's Order Number 11," *PAJHS* 40 (December 1950): 184–86; Korn, *American Jewry and the Civil War*, 140–43; *Israelite* 9 (February 6, 1863), 244; *PUSG* 7, p. 51n ("no orders authorizing or encouraging General Orders No. 11 have been found"); see Louis I. Newman, "David Eckstein," ms. 99 8/10, AJA, for the claim that Eckstein had seen the telegram to Grant; and for Rosewater's rebuttal, see *Omaha Bee* (July 27, 1885), 4; *American Israelite* (August 7, 1885), 4.

36. Eli Evans, "The War Between Jewish Brothers in America," in *Jews and the Civil War*, ed. Jonathan D. Sarna and Adam Mendelsohn (New York: New York University Press, 2010), 43–45; *Israelite* 15, no. 22 (December 4, 1868): 4; *Hamagid* 7 (February 12, 1863): 84; U. S. Grant to C. P. Wolcott (December 17, 1862) in *PUSG* 7, pp. 56–57; Cadwallader, *Three Years with Grant*, 22–23.

37. Much of our knowledge of this scheme comes from Jesse R. Grant's unsuccessful lawsuit against the Macks, reported in Cincinnati papers on May 17, 1864, and reprinted with minor differences in Matthew Carey Jr., comp., *The Democratic Speaker's*

Hand-book: Containing Every Thing Necessary for the Defense of the National Democracy in the Upcoming Presidential Campaign, and for the Assault of the Radical Enemies of the Country and Its Constitution, comp. Matthew Carey Jr. (Cincinnati: Miami Print and Publishing Company, 1868), 42–43 (available online at http://www.archive.org/details/democraticspeak00firgoog) and in *New York Daily Tribune* (September 19, 1872) (copy in AJA). Journalist Sylvanus Cadwallader, who was present when Jesse R. Grant visited, left an account in his manuscript memoirs, "Forty Years with Grant," 47–49, found in the Abraham Lincoln Presidential Library, Springfield, Illinois, which kindly provided me with a scan; most of the text is quoted in Earl Schenck Miers, *The Web of Victory* (New York: Alfred A. Knopf, 1955), 54–57, and in Korn, *American Jewry and the Civil War,* 277–78 (who dismissed the account). Another eyewitness, General James Harrison Wilson, provided a similar account (and a similar psychological explanation) in a late-nineteenth-century interview quoted in McFeely, *Grant,* 123–24. *PUSG* 7, p. 53, reviews other evidence; see also John Simon, "That Obnoxious Order," in *Jews and the Civil War: A Reader,* eds. Jonathan D. Sarna and Adam Mendelsohn (New York: New York University Press, 2010), 357–58; and, for background on Henry Mack, Michael W. Rich, "Henry Mack: An Important Figure in Nineteenth-Century American Jewish History," *AJA* 47 (1995): 261–79. Frankland, "Kronikals of the Times," 104, excoriates "David Mack" for misdeeds in Memphis and claims that he was in league with Jesse Grant.

38. Frederick D. Grant to Isaac Markens (December 8, 1907) in Isaac Markens, *Abraham Lincoln and the Jews* (New York: printed for the author, 1909), 16.

39. Grant, *The Personal Memoirs of Julia Dent Grant,* 107.

40. *Hamagid* 7 (February 12, 1863): 84, 131–32 (translation mine).

3. The Election of 1868

1. On Wolf, see Panitz, *Simon Wolf,* and John C. Livingston, "Wolf, Simon," http://www.anb.org/articles/08/08-01694.html; *American National Biography Online,* February 2000 (accessed December 7, 2009).

2. Simon Wolf, *Selected Addresses and Papers of Simon Wolf* (Cincinnati: Union of American Hebrew Congregations, 1926), 281.

3. *The History of Tuscarawas, County, Ohio . . .* (Chicago: Warner, Beers & Co., 1884), 378, online at http://www.heritagepursuit.com/Tuscarawas/TuscarawasChapIX.htm.

4. Wolf, *Presidents I Have Known,* quote is from p. 6; see Abigail Green, *Moses Montefiore: Jewish Liberator, Imperial Hero* (Cambridge, Mass.: Belknap Press of Harvard University Press, 2010), 134.

5. Ibid., 12; Wolf's letter was reprinted in *The Occident* 20 (February–March 1863): 496–97.

6. Wolf, *Presidents I Have Known*, 10–11; Korn, *American Jewry and the Civil War*, 169–71.

7. Grant's ascent may be traced through John Y. Simon's "Ulysses S. Grant Chronology," available online at http://library.msstate.edu/usgrant/chronology.asp (accessed December 8, 2009).

8. Wolf, *Presidents I Have Known*, 64.

9. Ibid.

10. *New York Herald* (April 13, 1841), 2; see Jonathan D. Sarna, *Jacksonian Jew: The Two Worlds of Mordecai Noah* (New York: Holmes & Meier, 1981), 101; William Prendergast, *The Catholic Voter in American Politics* (Washington, D.C.: Georgetown University Press, 1999), 37–41; Charles P. Connor, "Archbishop Hughes and Midcentury Politics, 1844–1860," *U.S. Catholic Historian* 3 (Fall–Winter 1983): 167–77.

11. William Pencak, *Jews and Gentiles in Early America, 1654–1800* (Ann Arbor: University of Michigan Press, 2005), 16–17, 133–34, 240–45.

12. Wolf, *Selected Addresses and Papers*, 104–5. When Wolf changed his mind and supported Grant, these words were used against him; see *New York Evening Express* as reprinted in *Daily Arkansas Gazette* (August 23, 1868), issue 218, col. E.

13. *Israelite* (February 28, 1868), 4; also reprinted in *Daily Arkansas Gazette* (March 8, 1868), col. B.

14. "General Grant and the Jews," *Flemingsburg Democrat* (March 6, 1868), online at http://alpha3.jtsa.edu:8997/aleph_images/naj/077_1868_0319_01a.pdf.

15. *New York World* (March 24, 1868) as quoted in Ph. Von Bort, *General Grant and the Jews* (New York: National News Company, 1868), 5; *Daily Memphis Avalanche* (March 10, 1868), 4; *St. Louis Dispatch*, as reprinted in the Savannah *Daily News and Herald* (March 24, 1868), col. B. Also see *Chicago Times* (September 18, 1868) and Joakim Isaacs, "Candidate Grant and the Jews," *AJA* 17 (1965):6, which takes the story at face value.

16. McFeely, *Grant*, 273.

17. Julia Dent Grant, *The Personal Memoirs of Julia Dent Grant*, ed. John Y. Simon (New York: Putnam, 1975), 171 (quoted); McFeely, *Grant*, 276–77; Martin E. Mantell, *Johnson, Grant and the Politics of Reconstruction* (New York: Columbia University Press, 1973), 97–100.

18. A facsimile of the statement may be found online at http://faculty.css.edu/mkelsey/usgrant/facs.html. Printed texts contain minor errors that I have corrected based on this original.

19. A. E. Frankland, "Kronikals of the Times—Memphis, 1862," *AJA* 9 (October 1957):104.

20. Von Bort, *General Grant and the Jews*, 16. The pamphlet is signed "A Jew," and the otherwise unknown "Ph. Von Bort" is apparently a pseudonym.

21. Mantell, *Johnson, Grant and the Politics of Reconstruction*, 113–28; more generally on the 1868 campaign, see John Hope Franklin, "Election of 1868," in *History of American Presidential Elections, 1789–1968*, ed. Arthur M. Schlesinger Jr. and Fred L. Israel, 4 vols. (New York: Chelsea House, 1971), 2:1247–1300, and Charles H. Cole-

man, *The Election of 1868: The Democratic Effort to Regain Control* (New York: Columbia University Press, 1933).

22. *The Democratic Speaker's Hand-book: Containing Every Thing Necessary for the Defense of the National Democracy in the Upcoming Presidential Campaign, and for the Assault of the Radical Enemies of the Country and Its Constitution,* comp. Matthew Carey Jr. (Cincinnati: Miami Printing and Publishing Company, 1868), available online at http://www.archive.org/details/democraticspeakoofirgoog), iii, 5; David Quigley, *Second Founding: New York City, Reconstruction and the Making of American Democracy* (New York: Hill and Wang, 2004), 44.

23. John A. Rawlins to Lewis N. Dembitz (May 6, 1868), published as "Gen. Grant and the Jews," *New York Times* (June 22, 1868), 5; *Boston Daily Advertiser* (June 23, 1868), issue 149, col. F; *Cincinnati Daily Gazette* (June 20, 1868), 2. On Rawlins and Dembitz, see *American National Biography.*

24. Adam Badeau to Simon Wolf (April 22, 1868), Simon Wolf Papers, AJHS, N.Y.; the letter is reprinted with slight punctuation changes in Wolf, *Presidents I Have Known,* 65–66.

25. Wolf, *Presidents I Have Known,* 63, 69, 70; Panitz, *Simon Wolf,* 34.

26. George S. Hellman, *The Story of the Seligmans* (typescript, Jacob R. Marcus Papers, box 476, AJA), I, 121a; Linton Wells, *The House of Seligman* (typescript, Collection 475, box 2, AJA), I, 132; Ross L. Muir and Carl J. White, *Over the Long Term: The Story of J. & W. Seligman & Co.* (New York: J. & W. Seligman, 1964), 38, 39, 42, 57.

27. *New York Times* (June 12, 1868), 5.

28. Joseph Medill to Elihu B. Washburne (June 16, 1868), Washburne Mss., Library of Congress, as reprinted in Isaacs, "Candidate Grant and the Jews," 9–10; *PUSG* 19, p. 20.

29. Isaacs, "Candidate Grant and the Jews," 9–10; U. S. Grant to I. N. Morris (September 14, 1868), *PUSG* 19, pp. 37–39; see also pp. 17–21 and 26–27.

30. Irving Katz, "Belmont, August," *American National Biography Online,* http://www.anb.org/articles/04/04–00092.html (accessed December 27, 2009); David Black, *The King of Fifth Avenue: The Fortunes of August Belmont* (New York: Dial Press, 1981), esp. 292–93.

31. *The Democratic Speaker's Hand-book,* 28–31, 34–35, 42–43; see also 380, 383.

32. The story ("Why Grant Dislikes the Jews") was published, among other places, in the *Israelite* (June 12, 1868), 2; *Daily Arkansas Gazette* (June 10, 1868), issue 155, col. B, and the *Salt Lake Daily Telegraph* (June 17, 1868), issue 298, col. A. Rosenthal's rejoinder ("Grant and the Jews—A Falsehood Exposed") was reprinted in the *Daily Cleveland Herald* (June 5, 1868), issue 135, col. C, and *The Daily Miners' Register* (June 13, 1868), issue 275, col. D.

33. *The Charleston Courier* (July 28, 1868), col. D.

34. *La Crosse Daily Democrat* (August 19, 1868), as quoted in Isaacs, "Candidate Grant and the Jews," 9.

35. Notes concerning the *Corinth Caucasian* I:1 (July 9, 1868), which recalled General Orders No. 11 in its very first issue, may be found in Bertram W. Korn Papers, box 6, AJA.

36. New York Democratic Platform as quoted in James M. McPherson, *Battle Cry of Freedom: The Civil War Era* (New York: Oxford University Press, 1988), 560; *The Lives of Horatio Seymour and Frank P. Blair: Campaign Edition* (Philadelphia: T. B. Peterson & Bros., 1868), 52, 61. The volume is available online at http://ia311303 .us.archive.org/3/items/livesofhoratioseoophil/livesofhoratioseoophil.pdf.

37. *The Lives of Horatio Seymour and Frank P. Blair*, 90.

38. The cartoon and an accompanying commentary may be found online at http:// blackhistory.harpweek.com/7Illustrations/Reconstruction/ThisIsAWhiteMans Gov.htm. Although most Irish allied with the Democrats, both parties actually engaged in ethnic appeals to them; see Coleman, *Election of 1868*, 302–4. Colfax's former ties to the anti-Catholic Know-Nothing Party were trumpeted by Democrats in a bid for Irish votes; see *The Democratic Speaker's Hand-book*, 44–45, 368.

39. The letter originally appeared in the *Boston Transcript* (August 6, 1868) and was reprinted in Little Rock's *Morning Republican* (August 22, 1868), *Milwaukee Daily Sentinel* (September 10, 1868), and "all over the United States"; see Wolf's *Presidents I Have Known*, 67–70.

40. *Boston Daily Advertiser* (August 18, 1868), issue 42, col. B.

41. London *Jewish Chronicle* (September 25, 1868), 2. Korn, *American Jewry and the Civil War*, 134, notes that Ezekiel's life was threatened after his letter appeared; *Hebrew Leader* (September 11, 1868), 4. On Moses Ezekiel, see Jonathan D. Sarna, *American Judaism: A History* (New Haven, Conn.: Yale University Press, 2004), 123–24.

42. "General Grant and the Jews," [Washington, D.C.] *Daily National Intelligencer* (July 25, 1868), issue 17,445, col. G; see Judy G. Ringel, *Children of Israel: The Story of Temple Israel, Memphis, Tennessee: 1854–2004* (Memphis: Temple Israel Books, 2004), 15. For Nashville, see Fedora S. Frank, "Nashville Jewry During the Civil War," *Tennessee Historical Quarterly* 39 (1980): 321–22; both gatherings were noticed in *The Democratic Speaker's Hand-book*, 380, 383.

43. Steven Hertzberg, *Strangers Within the Gate City: The Jews of Atlanta* (Philadelphia: Jewish Publication Society, 1978), 156. For St. Louis, see Adolph Moses's criticism of their meeting in *New York Times* (October 13, 1858), 1; for Los Angeles, see Max Vorspan and Lloyd P. Gartner, *History of the Jews of Los Angeles* (San Marino, Calif.: Huntington Library, 1970), 47–48, and Norton B. Stern, "Los Angeles Jewish Voters During Grant's First Presidential Race," *Western States Jewish Historical Quarterly* 13 (1981): 179–85.

44. See, generally, Jonathan D. Sarna and David G. Dalin, *Religion and State in the American Jewish Experience* (Notre Dame, Ind.: University of Notre Dame Press, 1997); and Bertram W. Korn, *The American Reaction to the Mortara Case, 1858–1859* (Cincinnati: AJA, 1957).

45. Moses Gaster, *History of the Ancient Synagogue of the Spanish and Portuguese Jews* (London: n.p., 1901), 88; *Kinship and Consent: The Jewish Political Tradition and Its Contemporary Uses*, ed. Daniel J. Elazar (Ramat Gan, Israel: Turtledove, 1981), esp. 273–75.

46. Naomi W. Cohen, *Encounter with Emancipation: The German Jews in the United States, 1830–1914* (Philadelphia: Jewish Publication Society, 1984), 129–58, esp. 129–30.

47. "General Grant and the Jews," [Washington, D.C.] *Daily National Intelligencer* (July 25, 1868), issue 17,445, col. G.

48. Cohen, *Encounter with Emancipation*, 129–58; for a parallel discussion concerning the attitudes toward politics of the great Jewish leader Louis Marshall, see David G. Dalin, "Louis Marshall, the Jewish Vote, and the Republican Party," *Jewish Political Studies Review* 4 (September 1992): 55–84.

49. Wolf, *Presidents I Have Known*, 67–70.

50. *Jewish Messenger* (June 5, 1868); *New York Times* (June 14, September 10, October 13, 1868); *Daily Cleveland Herald* (June 11, 1868).

51. Liebman Adler, "Grant and the Israelites, Views of Our Intelligent Hebrews," *Milwaukee Daily Sentinel* (August 7, 1868), issue 187, col. D. The article originally appeared in the *Illinois Staatszeitung* and was also reprinted in the *Missouri Democrat*. Isaacs, "Candidate Grant and the Jews," 12–13, did not realize that the article was by Liebman Adler. On Adler, see Joan Weil Saltzstein, ed., *Liebman Adler: His Life Through His Letters* (privately published, 1975), esp. 92.

52. "The General Grant Question," *Israelite* (June 26, 1868), 4, available online at http://www.americanjewisharchives.org/wise/attachment/3472/TIS-1868-06-26-001.pdf (accessed January 4, 2010).

53. The *Charleston Courier, Tri-Weekly* (July 28, 1868), col. D; London *Jewish Chronicle* (July 24, 1868); Cleveland *Plain Dealer* (October 20, 1868). Also quoted and rebutted in *Daily Cleveland Herald* (October 21, 1868), issue 241, col. B, and *St. Louis Times* as quoted in [Washington, D.C.] *Daily National Intelligencer* (October 24, 1868), issue 17,523, col. B.

54. *New York Times* (October 13, November 29, 1868); Wolf, *Presidents I Have Known*, 66; Korn, *American Jewry and the Civil War*, 135–36; *PUSG* 19, pp. 37–39. Congressman Morris explained to Isaac M. Wise that publication of the letter "during the pendency of the election would have cast suspicion on the motive which prompted it," *Israelite* (November 27, 1868), 4.

55. *New York Herald* (October 23, 1868); Korn, *American Jewry and the Civil War*, 137; Louis I. Newman, "David Eckstein," ms. 99 8/10, AJA; *PUSG* 19, pp. 25–27. The documents used by Newman suggest that Eckstein hoped for some "advantage" as reward for his efforts on Grant's behalf. On Eckstein, see *American Israelite* (March 15, 1878), 4, and Louis I. Newman, "Eckstein, David," *Universal Jewish Encyclopedia* (New York: Universal Jewish Encyclopedia, 1941), 3:622.

56. Coleman, *Election of 1868*, 384; Mantell, *Johnson, Grant and the Politics of Reconstruction*, 143–49; Franklin, "Election of 1868," 2:1265–66, 1300.

57. *Cleveland Herald* (December 2, 1869); *New York Times* (November 30, 1868), 4.
58. "Diary of Louis Ehrich," April 6, 1868, Sterling Memorial Library, Yale University, New Haven, Connecticut, as quoted in Jonathan D. Sarna, "A Jewish Student in Nineteenth-Century America: The Diary of Louis Ehrich—Yale '69," in *Jews in New Haven*, ed. Jonathan D. Sarna (New Haven, Conn.: Jewish Historical Society of New Haven, 1978), 75.
59. The letter was first published in the *Israelite* (November 27, 1868), 4, and I have used that text, complete with its original italicization. The *New York Times* (November 30, 1868) deleted the italics; see also *The Occident* 26 (December 1868): 440, and Grant's original text, without italics, in *PUSG* 19, p. 37.
60. *Israelite* (November 27, 1868), 4; *New York Times* (December 13, 1868), 3; *The Occident* 26 (December 1868): 440.
61. *New York Times* (November 30, 1868), 4; Sarna, *American Judaism*, 124–25.

4. "To Prove Impartiality Towards Israelites"

1. Brooks D. Simpson, *The Reconstruction Presidents* (Lawrence: University Press of Kansas, 1998), 133.
2. Grant's first inaugural address (March 4, 1869) may be found online at http://bartleby.com/124/pres33.html.
3. Heather Cox Richardson, "North and West of Reconstruction: Studies in Political Economy," in *Reconstructions: New Perspectives on the Post-Bellum United States*, ed. Thomas J. Brown (New York: Oxford University Press, 2006), 66–90, esp. 69; Eric Foner, *Reconstruction: America's Unfinished Revolution, 1863–1877* (New York: Harper & Row, 1988), 257.
4. Harry S. Stout, *Upon the Altar of the Nation: A Moral History of the American Civil War* (New York: Viking, 2006), 147; Morton Borden, *Jews, Turks and Infidels* (Chapel Hill: University of North Carolina Press, 1984), 58–74; Naomi W. Cohen, *Jews in Christian America* (New York: Oxford University Press, 1992), 65–72. Jim Allison, "The NRA and the Christian Amendment," http://candst.tripod.com/nra.htm (accessed February 1, 2010), reproduces the basic documents; see also *The Occident* 22 (January 1865): 433–45.
5. On Brown, see Kenneth H. Winn, "Brown, Benjamin Gratz," in *Dictionary of Missouri Biography* (Columbia: University of Missouri Press, 1999), 121–24, and Norma L. Peterson, *Freedom and Franchise: The Political Career of B. Gratz Brown* (Columbia: University of Missouri Press, 1965); quote is from *The Reformed Presbyterian and Covenanter* 4 (January 1866): 181.
6. *Proceedings of the National Convention to Secure the Religious Amendment of the Constitution . . . with an Account of the Origin and Progress of the Movement* (Philadelphia: James B. Rodgers Co., 1872), 8.

7. Borden, *Jews, Turks and Infidels*, 68.

8. *PUSG* 19, p. 19.

9. *Senate Executive Journal* 17 (April 17, 1869): 202; Panitz, *Simon Wolf*, 32–33. Panitz claims that this position was actually created for Wolf; however, Grant, in appointing Wolf, said that he was to replace Ohio attorney F. P. Cuppy, who had resigned.

10. Wolf, *Presidents I Have Known*, 72; *Senate Executive Journal* 17 (April 20, 1869): 229, 241; Panitz, *Simon Wolf*, 32–33.

11. Laurence F. Schmeckebier, *The District of Columbia: Its Government and Administration* (Baltimore: Johns Hopkins University Press, 1928), 707–9; Wolf, *Presidents I Have Known*, 71–73.

12. *New York Times* (October 23, 1921); Frederick Douglass, *Life and Times of Frederick Douglass, Written by Himself* (Boston: DeWolfe & Fiske Co., 1892), 639; Public Law 379, 82d Congress (66 Stat. 129).

13. Ross L. Muir and Carl J. White, *Over the Long Term: The Story of J. & W. Seligman & Co.* (New York: J. & W. Seligman, 1964), 57; Smith, *Grant*, 470; Joseph L. Grabill, "Straus, Oscar Solomon," http://www.anb.org/articles/06/06–00632.html, *American National Biography Online*, February 2000 (accessed February 18, 2010).

14. [N. Taylor Phillips?], "Solomons, Adolphus Simeon," Adolphus Simeon Solomons Papers, P-28, box 1, folder 1, AJHS; David de Sola Pool, "Adolphus Solomons," *Dictionary of American Biography*, ed. Dumas Malone (New York: Scribner, 1936), 9:393–94.

15. On Jewish appointments see, for example, *Israelite* (January 14, 1870), 10; (February 25, 1870), 9; (June 23, 1876), 5; (October 25, 1877), 5, and, for documents concerning Sterne, SC 12003, AJA. For the claim of "more than fifty appointments," see *American Hebrew* (October 20, 1916), 841, and Panitz, *Simon Wolf*, 35. The claim about Grant having appointed "more Israelites . . . than any other President" was first made in a toast in June 1870; see London *Jewish Chronicle* (June 15, 1870), 10.

16. Edmond S. Meany, *Governors of Washington, Territorial and State* (Seattle: Department of Printing, University of Washington, 1915), 43–44; Lee M. Friedman, *Jewish Pioneers and Patriots* (Philadelphia: Jewish Publication Society, 1942), 353–64; David Gleicher, "From Jewish Immigrant to Union General in Under Ten Years," *Chicago Jewish History* 15 (Winter 1992): 1, 8, 9; Alan Rabinowitz, "The Forgotten Governor of Washington Territory: Edward S. Salomon, 1870–1872," unpublished research note, AJA; *PUSG* 20, p. 351; Robert E. Ficken, "Figureheads of State," *Columbia Magazine* 19, no. 4 (Winter 2005–6), online at http://columbia.washingtonhistory.org/anthology/fromtriballands/figureheads.aspx (accessed February 25, 2010); "The Governor of Washington Territory, 1870–1872," *Western States Jewish History* 17 (1984):216n6; *Israelite* (January 14, 1870), 10 (italics added); *Archives Israelite* 31 (1870): 147.

17. *American Israelite* (October 27, 1871) as quoted in "The Governor of Washington Territory," 216n6.

18. Letter-report from R. H. Leipold from Olympia, W.T., to the Secretary of the Treasury, dated July 24, 1871, in File Microcopies of Records in the National Archives: no. 26, roll 2, State Department Territorial Papers, Washington Series, vol. 2 (February 18, 1859–December 4, 1872), National Archives (Washington, D.C., 1942), item 744; *PUSG* 20, pp. 351–52; Rabinowitz, "The Forgotten Governor," 2–3; Ficken, "Figureheads of State"; Mark W. Summers, *The Era of Good Stealings* (New York: Oxford University Press, 1993), 95–100, esp. 98.

19. Letter-report from R. H. Leipold from Olympia, W.T., to the Secretary of the Treasury, dated July 24, 1871; Rabinowitz, "The Forgotten Governor," 3; *PUSG* 20, pp. 351–52; Allan Nevins, *Hamilton Fish: The Inner History of the Grant Administration* (New York: Unger, 1957), 2:593 (quoting Fish's diary, January 9, 1872).

20. Simon Wolf, *The American Jew as Patriot, Soldier and Citizen* (Philadelphia: Levytype Company, 1895), 169; Nevins, *Hamilton Fish*, 2:593. Salomon subsequently moved to San Francisco and resumed his political career, serving as district attorney and as a California legislator; L. Sandy Maisel and Ira N. Forman, *Jews in American Politics* (Lanham, Md.: Rowman & Littlefield, 2001), 412.

21. Norton B. Stern, "Herman Bendell: Superintendent of Indian Affairs, Arizona Territory, 1871–1873," *Western States Jewish Historical Quarterly* 8 (1975–76):265–82; Abraham S. Chanin, "Herman Bendell," *Western States Jewish History* 31 (1999): 336–44.

22. The text of the inaugural address is available online at http://avalon.law.yale.edu/19th_century/grant1.asp (accessed March 11, 2010).

23. McFeely, *Grant*, 305–18; Smith, *Grant*, 515–41; Richard R. Levine, "Indian Fighters and Indian Reformers: U. S. Grant's Indian Peace Policy," *Civil War History* 31 (December 1985):329–52; Robert H. Keller, *American Protestantism and United States Indian Policy, 1869–82* (Lincoln: University of Nebraska Press, 1982); Francis P. Prucha, *American Indian Policy in Crisis: Christian Reformers and the Indian, 1865–1900* (Norman: University of Oklahoma Press, 1975).

24. On Parker, see William H. Armstrong, *Warrior in Two Camps: Ely S. Parker, Union General and Seneca Chief* (Syracuse, N.Y.: Syracuse University Press, 1978), 134–51, 176.

25. *PUSG* 21, p. 152; Levine, "Indian Fighters and Indian Reformers," 333; Francis P. Prucha, ed., *Documents of United States Indian Policy* (Lincoln: University of Nebraska Press, 2000), 132.

26. Keller, *American Protestantism and United States Indian Policy*, 34–35; Jonathan D. Sarna, "The American Jewish Response to Nineteenth-Century Christian Missions," *Journal of American History* 68 (June 1981): 35–51.

27. Wolf, *Presidents I Have Known*, 80–81; Keller, *American Protestantism and United States Indian Policy*, 261n46; *Jewish Times* (January 6, 1871), 712–13, as quoted in Stern, "Herman Bendell," 270.

28. Wolf, *Presidents I Have Known*, 80–81; Stern, "Herman Bendell," 269–70; *Senate Executive Journal* 19 (January 12, 1871): 606.

29. Stern, "Herman Bendell," 272–76; Bendell's reports are reprinted in *Western States Jewish History* 22 (1989–90): 195–206, 306–15, quote from 314–15.

30. Robert A. Trennert, "John H. Stout and the Grant Peace Policy Among the Pimas," *Arizona and the West* 28 (Spring 1986): 54, 56; Wolf, *Presidents I Have Known*, 81–82; Chanin, "Herman Bendell," 343; *Senate Executive Journal* 21 (March 25, 1873): 109. Tonner had previously been the Indian agent at the Colorado River indian reservation managed by the Dutch Reformed Church. See Stern, "Herman Bendell," 279, and *Annual Report of the Commissioner of Indian Affairs to the Secretary of the Interior for the Year 1875* (Washington, D.C.: Government Printing Office, 1875), 172, online at http://www.archive.org/stream/usindianaffairs75usdorich/ usindianaffairs75usdorich_djvu.txt (accessed March 11, 2010). In 1880, the Dutch Reformed Church acknowledged its failure in Indian affairs and withdrew from the field; see Keller, *American Protestantism and United States Indian Policy*, 62.

31. *Senate Executive Journal* 22 (December 3, 1873): 142.

5. "This Age of Enlightenment"

1. *New York Times* (November 27, 1869), 3.

2. David I. Kertzer, *The Kidnapping of Edgardo Mortara* (New York: Alfred A. Knopf, 1997), 127; Bertram W. Korn, *The American Reaction to the Mortara Case: 1858–1859* (Cincinnati: AJA, 1957).

3. Evelyn Levow Greenberg, "An 1869 Petition on Behalf of Russian Jews," *American Jewish Historical Quarterly* 54 (March 1965): 278–95; Eliyahu Feldman, "First Attempt of American Intervention on Behalf of the Russian Jews, 1869/70," *Zion* 30 (1965): 206–23 [in Hebrew]; Ronald J. Jensen, "The Politics of Discrimination: America, Russia, and the Jewish Question, 1869–1872," *American Jewish History* 75 (March 1986): 280–95.

4. The petition is printed in Greenberg, "An 1869 Petition," 280–281.

5. Schuyler's report is reprinted as an appendix to Feldman, "First Attempt," 220–21.

6. Wolf, *Presidents I Have Known*, 72–73; Diary of Hamilton Fish, November 30, 1869, as quoted in Jensen, "Politics of Discrimination," 282. A slightly different text of Grant's comments, from the *Washington Chronicle*, is quoted in *PUSG* 21, p. 76.

7. Greenberg, "An 1869 Petition," 285, 289; Feldman, "First Attempt," 212–15; Jensen, "Politics of Discrimination," 282–88.

8. Feldman, "First Attempt," 217–19, 222–23; *Jewish Times* (December 10, 1869), 6, as quoted in Greenberg, "An 1869 Petition," 283; *Charleston Courier Tri-Weekly* (December 7, 1869; reprinted from *New York World*); see *Daily Cleveland Herald* (December 2, 1869).

9. *New York Times* (June 14, 1867), 2.

10. Carol Iancu, "The Struggle for the Emancipation of Romanian Jewry and Its International Ramifications," in *The History of the Jews in Romania: The Nineteenth Century*, ed. Liviu Rotman and Carol Iancu (Tel Aviv: Goldstein-Goren Diaspora Research Center, 2005), 2:119–26, quote from 2:121; Max J. Kohler, "The Board of Delegates of American Israelites, 1859–1878," *PAJHS* 29 (1925):91–98.

11. [San Francisco] *Daily Evening Bulletin* (June 2, 1870); *New York Times* (June 3, 1870), 1; (June 5, 1870), 4; (June 6, 1870), 5; (June 9, 1870), 1; (June 15, 1870), 2); cf. *American Israelite* (June 10, 1870), 8.

12. *New York Times* (June 3, 1870), 1; (June 6, 1870), 5; Max J. Kohler and Simon Wolf, *Jewish Disabilities in the Balkan States* (New York: American Jewish Committee, 1916), 8.

13. *New York Times* (June 3, 1870), 1; Lloyd P. Gartner, *American and British Jews in the Age of the Great Migration* (London: Vallentine Mitchell, 2009), 171 (Gartner's article earlier appeared in *American Jewish Historical Quarterly* 58 [1968]: 25–117).

14. Kohler and Wolf, *Jewish Disabilities in the Balkan States*, 2.

15. David Assaf, *Caught in the Thicket: Chapters of Crisis and Discontent in the History of Hasidism* (Jerusalem: Mercaz Shazar, 2006), 70n69 [in Hebrew]; David Assaf, *Untold Tales of the Hasidim* (Waltham, Mass.: Brandeis University Press, 2010), 76; Shalom D. Levin, *Toildois Chabad B'Eretz Ha'Koidesh* (Brooklyn, N.Y.: Kehot, 1988), 78 [in Hebrew].

16. Israel Klausner, *Rabbi Hayyim Zvi Sneersohn* (Jerusalem: Mosad Harav Kook, 1973) [in Hebrew]; H. Z. Sneersohn, *Palestine and Roumania: A Description of the Holy Land and the Past and Present State of Roumania, and the Roumanian Jews* (New York: Arno, 1977 [1872]).

17. Sneersohn, *Palestine and Roumania*, xii, xiv; Klausner, *Rabbi Hayyim Zvi Sneersohn*, 62; *San Francisco Daily Evening Bulletin* (May 20, 1870); Norton B. Stern and William M. Kramer, "A Pre-Israeli Diplomat on an American Mission, 1869–1870," *Western States Jewish Historical Quarterly* 8 (1976): 232–42; Ruth Kark, *American Consuls in the Holy Land, 1832–1914* (Jerusalem: Magnes Press, 1994), 159, 213, 315–17; Mordecai Eliav, "The Sarah Steinberg Affair," *Sinai* 64 (1969): 78–91 [in Hebrew].

18. *New York Times* (February 19, 1869).

19. Sneersohn, Palestine and Roumania, xii, 85–86; *PUSG* 19, pp. xxiv, 436; Klausner, *Rabbi Hayyim Zvi Sneersohn*, 64–67; [London] *Jewish Chronicle* (May 26, 1869), 13; *Archives Israelites* 30 (1869): 375–77; Yitzchok Levine, "The Jerusalem Rabbi Who Met President Ulysses S. Grant," http://personal.stevens.edu/~llevine/sneersohn .pdf (accessed March 28, 2010); prayer for the president retranslated according to Jonathan Saxe, *The Koren Sidder* (Jerusalem: Koren, 2009), 1002.

20. Lloyd P. Gartner, "Peixotto," *EJ*, 15:713; Lloyd P. Gartner, "Peixotto, Benjamin Franklin," http://www.anb.org/articles/04/04–00771.html; *American National*

Biography Online, February 2000 (accessed March 28, 2010); Albert A. Woldman, "A Hard-Hitting Leader," *National Jewish Monthly* (November 1940): 82–83; unpublished biographical sketch of Peixotto, Philip Lax Archive, B'nai B'rith, Washington, D.C.

21. Benjamin F. Peixotto to Myer Isaacs (June 7, 28, 1870), Board of Delegates of American Israelite Papers, AJHS, reprinted in Ava F. Kahn, ed., *Jewish Voices of the California Gold Rush: A Documentary History*, 1849–1880 (Detroit: Wayne State University Press, 2002), 479–83; Kohler and Wolf, *Jewish Disabilities in the Balkan States*, 10–11.

22. Sneersohn to Grant (January 19, 1870) in Sneersohn, *Palestine and Roumania*, 86–89; Wolf to Peixotto (June 14, 1870) in Gartner, *American and British Jews in the Age of the Great Migration*, 177; *New York Times* (December 12, 1868); *Senate Executive Journal* 19 (June 17, 1870): 479–81, (June 29, 1870): 499 (the name was consistently misspelled as "Piexotto"); *Israelite* (June 24, 1870).

23. Gartner, *American and British Jews in the Age of the Great Migration*, 180.

24. The text in Benjamin F. Peixotto, "Story of the Roumanian Mission," *The Menorah* 1 (1886): 26, which is quoted here, is practically identical to the text in Wolf, *Presidents I Have Known*, 74–75.

25. *PUSG* 21, p. 74; the handwritten original is in the AJHS, New York.

26. Benjamin F. Peixotto to Joseph Seligman (January 4, 1871), SC-9476, AJA.

27. *PUSG* 21, p. 77.

28. Ibid.; Panitz, *Simon Wolf*, 41–51.

29. B. F. Peixotto to A[lbert] Cohn (April 21, 1872) in Carol Iancu, "Benjamin Franklin Peixotto, L'Alliance israélite universelle et les Juifs de Roumanie: Correspondance inédite (1871–1876)," *Revue des Etudes Juives* 137 (January–June 1978): 77–147, quote from 126; Carol Iancu, *Les Juifs en Roumanie 1866–1919* (Provence: Editions de l'Université de Provence, 1978), 106–18; Gartner, *American and British Jews in the Age of the Great Migration*, 183–230; Lloyd P. Gartner, "Documents on Roumanian Jewry: Consul Peixotto and Jewish Diplomacy, 1870–1875," in *Salo Wittmayer Baron Jubilee Volume* (New York: Columbia University Press, 1974), 1:467–90; Benjamin F. Peixotto, "The Story of the Roumanian Mission," *The Menorah* 1–4 (1886–1888), *passim*.

30. *PUSG* 28, p. 69; Joan Waugh, *U. S. Grant: American Hero, American Myth* (Chapel Hill: University of North Carolina Press, 2009), 137; Benjamin F. Peixotto to A[lbert] Cohn (September 20, 1872) in Iancu, "Benjamin Franklin Peixotto," 133.

31. Gartner, *American and British Jews in the Age of the Great Migration*, 29–52, 201–10, quotes from 202–3; Sneersohn, *Palestine and Roumania*, 166; Klausner, *Rabbi Hayyim Zvi Sneersohn*, 98–103; Leon Horowitz, *Romaniah va-'Amerikah* (Berlin: n.p., 1874); *Israelite* (November 15, 1872); *Hamagid* 16 (December 11, 1872): 518; *North American and United States Gazette* (November 4, 1872); *Cleveland Morning Daily Herald* (October 16, 1872); Iancu, "Benjamin Franklin Peixotto," 91–95.

32. Adolphus Solomons to Myer Isaacs (May 9, 1872), Board of Delegates of American Israelites Papers, AJHS.

33. *Daily Arkansas Gazette* (July 16, 1872); William Shakespeare, *The Merchant of Venice*, act 1, scene 3; the Morgan cartoon was graciously made available to me by Arnold Kaplan, from the Arnold and Deanne Kaplan American Judaica Collection. For the Nast cartoon, see *Harper's Weekly* (July 6, 1872), 528, available online at http://elections.harpweek.com/1872/cartoon-1872-large.asp?UniqueID=22&Year=1872.

34. Israelite (July 12, 1872); *Jewish Messenger* (August 2, 1872); *Hebrew Leader*, as quoted in *North American and United States Gazette* (August 1, 1872); *New York Times* (August 25, 1872).

35. Smith, *Grant*, 552; George Templeton Strong, as quoted in William Gillette, "Election of 1872," in *History of American Presidential Elections, 1789–1968*, ed. Arthur M. Schlesinger Jr. and Fred L. Israel, 4 vols. (New York: Chelsea House, 1971), 2:1316; Grant, as quoted in McFeely, *Grant*, 384.

36. Smith, *Grant*, 552; *American Israelite* (July 7, 1876), 4.

37. Benny Kraut, "Frances E. Abbot: Perceptions of a Nineteenth-Century Religious Radical on Jews and Judaism," in *Studies in the American Jewish Experience*, ed. J. R. Marcus and A. J. Peck (Cincinnati: AJA, 1981), 99–101.

38. David Philipson, *Max Lilienthal* (New York: Bloch Publishing, 1915), 456–57, cf. 109–25.

39. *PUSG* 22, p. 394. Jesse Lilienthal never attended West Point.

40. *PUSG* 26, p. 344; http://www.infoplease.com/t/hist/state-of-the-union/87.html; James S. Clarkson, "General Grant's Des Moines Speech," *The Century Magazine* 55 (March 1898): 785–89.

41. *American Israelite* (November 9, 1875), 5; Smith, *Grant*, 569–71; Tyler Anbinder, "Ulysses S. Grant, Nativist," *Civil War History* 43 (June 1997): 119–42.

42. Stanley Rabinowitz, *The Assembly: A Century in the Life of the Adas Israel Hebrew Congregation of Washington, D.C.* (Hoboken, N.J.: Ktav, 1993), esp. 32–33; see *Journal of the Senate*, 34th Congress, 1st Session (June 10, 1856): 373. On European synagogue dedications attended by leaders, see, for example, Carol H. Krinsky, *Synagogues of Europe: Architecture, History, Meaning* (Cambridge, Mass.: MIT Press, 1985), 265.

43. Rabinowitz, *The Assembly*, 143–46; *American Israelite* (June 23, 1876), 5; *London Jewish Chronicle* (June 30, 1876), 196; PUSG 27, p. 161.

44. *American Israelite* (July 21, 1876), 5; (July 28, 1876), 4; Wolf, *Presidents I Have Known*, 88; Steven A. Fox, "On the Road to Unity: The Union of American Hebrew Congregations and American Jewry, 1873–1903," *AJA* 32 (November 1980): 145–93.

45. *The New Era* 1 (October 1870): 1–2; Isidor Kalisch, *Studies in Ancient and Modern Judaism* (New York: Dobsevage, 1928), 61; Jonathan D. Sarna, *American Judaism: A History* (New Haven, Conn.: Yale University Press, 2004), 124–34.

46. Wolf, *Presidents I Have Known*, 71.

6. "Then and Now"

1. McFeely, *Grant*, 450; Michael Fellman, "Introduction," in John Russell Young, *Around the World with General Grant* (Baltimore: Johns Hopkins University Press, 2002), xi–xix; *PUSG* 28, p. 333; Smith, *Grant*, 607.

2. W. H. Hicks, *General Grant's Tour Around the World* (Chicago: Rand McNally, 1879), 57, 77; Ross L. Muir and Carl J. White, *Over the Long Term: The Story of J. & W. Seligman & Co.* (New York: J. & W. Seligman, 1964), 58, 81; George S. Hellman, *The Story of the Seligmans* (typescript, Jacob R. Marcus Papers, box 476, AJA) I, 124 (quoted); *PUSG* 28, p. 242.

3. Adam Badeau, *Grant in Peace* (Hartford, Conn.: Scranton & Co., 1887), 299; *New York Times* (June 19, 1877; August 25, 1899); Beth S. Wenger, *The Jewish Americans: Three Centuries of Jewish Voices in America* (New York: Doubleday, 2007), 86.

4. Leonard Dinnerstein, *Antisemitism in America* (New York: Oxford University Press, 1994), 40; *Coney Island and the Jews* (New York: G. W. Carleton, 1879); Michael Seltzer, ed., *Kike! A Documentary History of Anti-Semitism in America* (New York: Meridian, 1972), 56.

5. Hilton Obenzinger, *American Palestine: Melville, Twain, and the Holy Land Mania* (Princeton, N.J.: Princeton University Press, 1999); Mark Twain [Samuel Clemens], *Innocents Abroad* (Charlottesville: Electronic Text Center, University of Virginia Library, 1996), 560, 606, available at http://etext.lib.virginia.edu/modeng/modeng0.browse.html (accessed June 30, 2010); Brian Yothers, *The Romance of the Holy Land in American Travel Writing, 1890–1876* (Burlington, Vt.: Ashgate, 2007); Michael Oren, *Power, Faith and Fantasy: America in the Middle East, 1776 to the Present* (New York: W. W. Norton, 2007), 228–45.

6. *PUSG* 28, p. 349; 29, p. 231.

7. *PUSG* 28, p. 350; Julia Dent Grant, *The Personal Memoirs of Julia Dent Grant*, ed. John Y. Simon (New York: Putnam, 1975), 235; J. F. Packard, *Grant's Tour Around the World* (Cincinnati: Forshee & McMakin, 1880), 317; John Russell Young, *Around the World with General Grant* (New York: American News Company, 1879), 340.

8. *PUSG* 28, p. 349; Lester I. Vogel, *To See a Promised Land: America and the Holy Land in the Nineteenth Century* (University Park: Pennsylvania State University Press, 1993), 148–52; on Floyd, see Reed M. Holmes, *The Forerunners* (Independence, Mo.: Herald Publishing, 1981), 171, 247, 252–54, 258–60, and Reed M. Holmes, *Dreamers of Zion: Joseph Smith and George J. Adams* (Portland, Ore.: Sussex Academic Press, 2003), esp. 152.

9. *New York Herald* (March 18, 1878), as reprinted in *PUSG* 28, p. 349; Simcha Fishbane, "The Founding of the Kollel America Tifereth Yerushalayim," *American Jewish Historical Quarterly* 64 (June 1974): 120–21. Earlier, in 1877, Russian Jews in Jerusalem had written to President Rutherford B. Hayes for help and protection; see Dov Genachowski, "Russian Immigrants in Jerusalem Write to the President of

the United States [in the 19th Century]," in *Mincha le-Menachem: A Collection of Essays in Honor of Rabbi Menachem Hacohen,* ed. Hana Amit, Aviad Hacohen, and Haim Beer (Tel Aviv: Kibbutz Hameuchad, 2007), 301–6 [in Hebrew].

10. Wolf, *Presidents I Have Known,* 94–95.

11. James D. McCabe, *A Tour Around the World by General Grant* (Philadelphia: National Publishing Company, 1879), 21; Badeau, *Grant in Peace,* 318; Smith, *Grant,* 617.

12. Stephen Birmingham, *Our Crowd* (New York: Harper & Row, 1967), 296n; *New York Times* (April 29, 1892), 9; Smith, *Grant,* 619.

13. Jonathan D. Sarna, *American Judaism: A History* (New Haven, Conn.: Yale University Press, 2004), 152; *Jewish Messenger* (July 31, 1885), 4; *PUSG* 30, p. 75; *New York Times* (February 2, 1882), 8; *Proceedings of Meetings Held February 1st, 1882, at New York and London, to Express Sympathy with the Oppressed Jews in Russia* (New York: Hebrew Orphans Asylum Press, 1882), 3.

14. *New York Times* (February 2, 1882), 8; *Proceedings of Meetings Held February 1st, 1882, at New York and London, to Express Sympathy with the Oppressed Jews in Russia,* esp. 3, 26 [this published text changed Newman's statement to "will give significance and potency to our utterances"]; *Jewish Encyclopedia* 9:279; Jonathan D. Sarna and Adam Mendelsohn, eds., *Jews and the Civil War: A Reader* (New York: New York University Press, 2010), 407.

15. *PUSG* 31, pp. 343–44; *Jewish Record* (August 7, 1885), 3; Janice Rothschild Blumberg, "Browne and Grant," unpublished manuscript in author's possession.

16. *PUSG* 31, pp. 392, 414; Badeau, *Grant at Peace,* 591.

17. [Philadelphia] *Jewish Record* (July 24, 1885), 4.

18. *Jewish Record* (July 31, 1885); *American Israelite* (July 31, 1885). On Chumaceiro, see Henry S. Morais, *Jews of Philadelphia* (Philadelphia: The Levytype Company, 1894), 106.

19. *Jewish Record* (August 14, 21, 1885); *Hamagid* 29 (August 20, 1885):288, as translated in *Jewish Record* (September 18, 1885), 8; *Jewish Messenger* (July 31, 1885), 4. On Montefiore, see Abigail Green, *Moses Montefiore: Jewish Liberator, Imperial Hero* (Cambridge, Mass.: Belknap Press of Harvard University Press, 2010), and Moshe Davis, *Sir Moses Montefiore: American Jewry's Ideal* (Jerusalem: American Jewish Archives in Israel, 1985).

20. Green, *Moses Montefiore,* esp. 321, 422; Isaac M. Wise, "A Record of Judaism for A. M. 5646," *American Jews Annual* 5647 (Cincinnati: Bloch, 1886), 61.

21. *American Israelite* (July 31, 1885); *Jewish Record* (August 14, 1885), 5, 8.

22. I am indebted to Janice Rothschild Blumberg, Browne's great-granddaughter, for much of what follows concerning Browne. In addition to her unpublished writings, which she has generously shared with me, see her "Rabbi Alphabet Browne: The Atlanta Years," *Southern Jewish History* 5 (2003):1–42; "Sophie Weil Browne: From Rabbi's Wife to Clubwoman," *Southern Jewish History* 9 (2006): 1–33; and "Voices for Justice: Rabbi Jacob M. Rothschild in Atlanta (1946–1973) and Edward B. M.

Browne in New York (1881–1889)," online at http://spinner.cofc.edu/~jwst/
pages/Blumberg,%20Janice%20-%20VOICES%20FOR%20JUSTICE%20++
.pdf?referrer=webcluster& (accessed July 5, 2010).

23. *PUSG* 22, p. 397.

24. *PUSG* 26, p. 280; Korn, *American Jewry and the Civil War*, 279n70.

25. The widely reprinted article appeared, among other places, in the [Washington]
Sunday Herald (July 26, 1885); [St. Paul] *Sunday Globe* (July 26, 1885); [Sacramento]
Day Record Union (July 27, 1885); and [Fort Worth] *Texas Gazette* (July 27, 1885).

26. Korn, *American Jewry and the Civil War*, 279; Frederick D. Grant to Isaac Markens
(December 8, 1907) in Isaac Markens, *Abraham Lincoln and the Jews* (New York:
printed for the author, 1909), 16; *Omaha Bee* (July 27, 1885), 4; *American Israelite*
(August 7, 1885), 4.

27. *New York Sun* (August 5, 1885); *Jewish Messenger* (July 31, 1885), 4; (August 7, 1885), 2.

28. John M. Thayer in *Omaha Bee* (August 6, 1885); on Thayer, see *PUSG* 21, p. 102;
Grant, *The Personal Memoirs of Julia Dent Grant*, 107.

29. *New York Times* (August 3, 1885); *Jewish Record* (August 14, 1885); *American Israelite*
(August 14, 1885).

30. *New York Times* (August 5, 6, 1885); Blumberg, "Voices for Justice," 7–8 (which
quotes both the telegram and the *Daily Graphic* [August 8, 1885]).

31. *New York Times* (August 9, 1913); *Grant We Are Here Again: Thirty-Fifth Memorial
Services for General Grant* (August 15, 1920), New York Public Library (a copy was
graciously provided to me by Roberta Saltzman).

32. Joan Waugh, *U. S. Grant: American Hero, American Myth* (Chapel Hill: University
of North Carolina, 2009), 284; *New York Times* (April 25, 1897); Uriel Rappaport,
"Hadrian, Publius Aelius," *EJ* 8:193–94.

33. [Pittsburgh] *Jewish Criterion* (April 30, 1897); *Jewish Messenger* (April 30, 1897); *New
York Times* (April 25, 1897).

34. Waugh, *U. S. Grant*, 303–8; Nicholas Leman, *Redemption: The Last Battle of the Civil
War* (New York: Farrar, Straus and Giroux, 2006), 190–209. For a helpful chart of
historical rankings of the presidents (1948–2010), see http://en.wikipedia.org/
wiki/Historical_rankings_of_Presidents_of_the_United_States.

35. Rufus Learsi [Israel Goldberg], *The Jews in America: A History* (New York: Ktav,
1972; orig. ed. 1954), 109; Frederick Cople Jaher, *A Scapegoat in the New Wilderness:
The Origins and Rise of Anti-Semitism in America* (Cambridge, Mass.: Harvard University
Press, 1994), 198–99; Dinnerstein, *Antisemitism in America*, 32; Bertram W.
Korn, "Grant, Ulysses Simpson," *EJ* 8:34.

36. Sean Wilentz, "The Return of Ulysses S. Grant," *The New Republic* (January 25, 2010); Sean Wilentz, "Who's Buried in the History Books," *New York Times*
(March 13, 2010); http://en.wikipedia.org/wiki/Historical_rankings_of_Presidents
_of_the_United_States.

ACKNOWLEDGMENTS

Anyone who writes about Ulysses S. Grant owes a primary debt of gratitude to the late John Y. Simon, who edited all thirty-one volumes of the invaluable work *The Papers of Ulysses S. Grant*, and also directed the Ulysses S. Grant Association, and published an important article on General Orders No. 11. While I did not know Professor Simon personally, I am the beneficiary of his prodigious scholarship. His successor, John F. Marszalek, has overseen the creation of an online digital collection of the Grant Papers as part of the Ulysses S. Grant Digital Collection at Mississippi State University. Having made substantial use of that collection, I am particularly grateful to the Ulysses S. Grant Association for establishing it.

The availability of online digital collections made it possible for me to write the bulk of this volume during a sabbatical in Jerusalem, where I served as Senior Scholar at the Mandel Leadership Institute. Annette Hochstein, Eli Gottlieb, Daniel Marom, Abigail Dauber-Sterne, and the entire staff of the institute made my year both enjoyable and productive. I hope that this book explains to my Mandel colleagues in Israel why the subject of Ulysses S. Grant and the Jews so fascinated me.

Prior to leaving for Jerusalem, I embarked upon highly productive research trips to the Jacob Rader Marcus Center of the American Jewish Archives in Cincinnati and to the American Jewish Historical Society in New York. Gary P. Zola, Kevin Proffitt, and the entire staff of the Marcus Center greatly assisted my research, taking hours away from their own duties to advance my work. Later, the superb staff also answered several research questions that I directed to them from afar and scanned rare documents for me to examine up close. I am enormously grateful for their longtime friendship.

Evan Kingsley, then director of the American Jewish Historical Society, along with his staff, also put themselves out on my behalf. I have been associated with the society since my undergraduate days and have learned an enormous amount under its tutelage. While the Center for Jewish History in New York, where the society is now located, represents a most impressive achievement, I still miss not having the archive nearby on the Brandeis campus.

This project gave me the opportunity to visit, for the first time, the Philip Lax Archive in Washington, which holds the archival records of B'nai B'rith. Daniel S. Mariaschin, executive vice president of B'nai B'rith International, and archivist Cheryl Kempler displayed great interest in my work and helped me uncover significant material that I might not otherwise have located.

Closer to home, the staff of the Brandeis University library, especially its interlibrary loan department, worked hard on my behalf. Brandeis has been deeply supportive of my scholarship for two full decades. I am glad to take this opportunity to thank the administration, as well as my colleagues and staff members in the Department of Near Eastern and Judaic Studies, the Hornstein Jewish Professional Leadership Program, and the History Department. In addition, I thank Dr. Bernard G. and Rhoda G. Sarnat, who established the Bernard G. and Rhoda G. Sarnat Center for the Study of Anti-Jewishness, which I direct, and Lawrence E. and Nancy S. Glick, who made the Joseph H. and Belle R. Braun Chair in American Jewish history possible in the first place.

Friends and colleagues from around the world helped me with the research on this book. James Ramage generously shared with me his entire file on General Orders No. 11. Arnold Kaplan sent me rare documents from his own private collection, including a cartoon that is published here with his permission. Israel Bartal, Janice Blumberg, David Dalin, Ellen Eisenberg, David Hackett Fischer, David Geffen, Menachem Genack, David Gleicher, Shira M. Kohn, Joshua Perelman, and William Toll answered questions, offered suggestions, and in some cases alerted me to sources that I had not previously uncovered. Together, they have strengthened this book immeasurably.

Through the years, talented Brandeis University students have served as research assistants or have otherwise had occasion to comment on my chapters-in-progress. I particularly thank Shimrit Hait, Gideon Klionsky, Mina Muraoka, Amaryah Orenstein, Rachel Salston, and my students in NEJS 162b, who spent a full month studying General Orders No. 11 and never complained.

Generous friends read and commented on earlier versions of these chapters. Deborah Block, T. Forcht Dagi, David Dalin, Carolyn Hessel, Shalom Lamm, Eran Shalev, Ellen Smith, and my brother, David E. Y. Sarna, all made invaluable suggestions that improved my writing and my thinking. Since I was by no means able to heed all of their sensible suggestions, the responsibility for errors and omissions remains mine alone.

My wife, Ruth Langer, did not read the manuscript of this book. She has been writing a much more ambitious tome that covers an almost-two-thousand-year span of Jewish history. But if Ruth and I have not exchanged chapters, we have regularly exchanged ideas. Our almost daily walks, and the many satisfactions that come from a quarter century of marriage, have enriched not only this book but every aspect of my life.

Our children, Aaron and Leah, have likewise enriched every aspect of my life. While they, too, did not read this book in manuscript, they have endured hearing about it on many of their visits home. They know how much pride I take in all of their achievements.

Last but not least, I thank my editor and childhood neighbor, Jonathan Rosen. His boundless enthusiasm for this project, along with his insightful suggestions and careful reading, improved each of my chapters in turn. I am proud that he made a place for this volume in his distinguished Nextbook series, and am grateful that it could be published to coincide with the anniversary of that day in 1862 "when General Grant expelled the Jews."

INDEX

Page numbers in *italics* refer to illustrations.

Index

Index

ILLUSTRATION CREDITS

73 Collection of the author.

81 Courtesy of the Library of Congress, LC-USZ62–4912 (http://www.loc.gov/ pictures/item/2001695231/).

82 Courtesy of the Library of Congress, LC-USZ62–90757 (http://www.loc.gov/ pictures/item/96515647).

88 Courtesy B'nai B'rith Klutznick National Jewish Museum, Adolphus Solomons Collection.

90 Courtesy of the Jacob Rader Marcus Center of the American Jewish Archives, Cincinnati, Ohio, americanjewisharchives.org.

93 Courtesy of Wikimedia Commons (http://upload.wikimedia.org/wikipedia/ commons/5/51/Ely_S._Parker.jpg).

96 From Harold W. Cole and Theodore C. Hailes, *The Public Schools of Albany: A Souvenir Volume* (Albany: Weed Parsons Printing, 1894), p.19.

107 From H. Z. Sneersohn, *Palestine and Roumania* (New York: Hebrew Orphan Asylum Printing Establishment, 1872), frontispiece.

109 Courtesy of the Jacob Rader Marcus Center of the American Jewish Archives, Cincinnati, Ohio, americanjewisharchives.org.

117 Courtesy of the Arnold and Deanne Kaplan American Judaica Collection.

122 Courtesy the District of Columbia Public Library, Washingtoniana Division.

127 Courtesy of the Library of Congress, LC-USZ62–55262 (http://www.loc.gov/ pictures/item/2004674979/).

128 From John R. Young, *Around the World with General Grant* (New York: The American News Company, 1879), p. 272.

133 Courtesy of the Library of Congress, LC-DIG-ppmsca-05643 (http://www.loc .gov/pictures/item/2004672483/).

141 Courtesy of the Library of Congress, LC-USZ62–74482 (http://www.loc.gov/ pictures/item/2003677344)

143 Courtesy of Janice R. Blumberg.

144 Courtesy of the Library of Congress, LC-USZ62–51512 (http://www.loc.gov/ pictures/item/2006678041/).

145 Courtesy of the Library of Congress, LC-USZC4–2437 (http://www.loc.gov/ pictures/item/93503161).